REVISE PEARSON EDEXCEL GCSE (9–1)

History

CRIME AND PUNISHMENT IN BRITAIN, c1000–present

PRACTICE PAPER Plus+

Series Consultant: Harry Smith

Author: Ben Armstrong

This Practice Paper is designed to complement your revision and to help you prepare for the exam. It does not include all the content and skills you need for the complete course and has been written to help you practise what you have learned. It may not be representative of a real exam paper. Remember that the official Pearson specification and associated assessment guidance materials are the only authoritative source of information and you should always refer to them for definitive guidance.

For further information, go to: **quals.pearson.com/GCSEHistory**

Published by Pearson Education Limited, 80 Strand, London, WC2R 0RL.
www.pearsonschoolsandfecolleges.co.uk

Copies of official specifications for all Pearson qualifications may be found on the website: qualifications.pearson.com

Produced, typeset and illustrated by QBS Learning
Cover illustration by Eoin Coveney

The rights of Ben Armstrong to be identified as author of this work have been asserted by him in accordance with the Copyright, Designs and Patents Act 1988.

First published 2020

23 22 21 20
10 9 8 7 6 5 4 3 2 1

British Library Cataloguing in Publication Data
A catalogue record for this book is available from the British Library

ISBN 978 1 292 31019 0

Printed in Slovakia by Neografia

Acknowledgements
Photographs:
123RF: johan2011 23, **Getty Images:** duncan1890/DigitalVision Vectors 13, 61.

Text Credits:
P61 Crown Copyright: Part of a letter from James Munro, Head of the CID to the Home Secretary, 11 Sept 1889, National Archives, © Crown Copyright. Contains public sector information licensed under the Open Government Licence v3.0.

Notes from the publisher
1. While the publishers have made every attempt to ensure that advice on the qualification and its assessment is accurate, the official specification and associated assessment guidance materials are the only authoritative source of information and should always be referred to for definitive guidance. Pearson examiners have not contributed to any sections in this resource relevant to examination papers for which they have responsibility.

2. Pearson has robust editorial processes, including answer and fact checks, to ensure the accuracy of the content in this publication, and every effort is made to ensure this publication is free of errors. We are, however, only human, and occasionally errors do occur. Pearson is not liable for any misunderstandings that arise as a result of errors in this publication, but it is our priority to ensure that the content is accurate. If you spot an error, please do contact us at resourcescorrections@pearson.com so we can make sure it is corrected.

Contents

About this book

This book is designed to help you prepare for your Pearson Edexcel GCSE (9–1) History Crime and punishment in Britain, c1000–present exam. It focuses on the skills you will need to answer the exam questions successfully.

You could work through the book in order. Alternatively, you could go straight to the section you want to focus on.

This Practice Paper Plus book

1 Knowledge booster
- ✓ Get started with these quick, warm-up activities
- ✓ Recap what you already know about the topic
- ✓ Find out what you need to revise in more detail
- ✓ Use the links to the Revise Pearson Edexcel GCSE (9–1) History Revision Guide and Workbook to find more revision support

2 Exam skills
- ✓ Get useful tips and guidance on how the exam works and what you need to do
- ✓ Understand how each question type works
- ✓ See how to write a successful answer with the 'steps to success' skills builders
- ✓ Learn how to avoid common mistakes

3 Practice paper
- ✓ Write straight into this book
- ✓ Have a go at a full practice paper on this topic
- ✓ Use the hints and reminders in the margins to stay focused on what you need to do to answer each question successfully
- ✓ Tackle the paper under exam conditions by covering up the guidance in the margins

4 Practice paper answers
- ✓ Read the mark schemes and notes to find out what a successful answer would include
- ✓ See full example answers to each question
- ✓ Look at the annotations and comments to understand what makes each answer successful
- ✓ Get ideas about how to improve your own responses in the exam

Medieval England

This key topic is about crime and punishment in medieval England from c1000 to c1500. It covers the nature and definitions of criminal activity and the nature of law enforcement and punishment in this period.

The nature of crime in medieval England

1 Give **one** example of a crime against the person.

....

2 Give **two** examples of crimes against property.

- ....
- ....

3 The most serious crimes were crimes against authority. Name **one** crime against authority.

....

4 Tick (✓) the correct definition of a social crime.

A. An unpopular crime.	☐	**C.** A crime shared on social media.	☐
B. A crime that most people do not disapprove of.	☐	**D.** A crime by rich people.	☐

5 Give **two** examples of ways that William I's Forest Laws affected Anglo-Saxons.

- ....
- ....

6 Define the term **murdrum fine**.

....

....

Law enforcement in Anglo-Saxon England

7 Draw lines to match the key terms on the left to the definitions on the right.

A. Tithing	**i.** A person could swear before God that they were innocent.
B. Hue and cry	**ii.** A witness to a crime had to shout to alert others.
C. Oath	**iii.** A group of men. Each one was responsible for any crimes committed by the others.
D. Court	**iv.** A local man appointed to take criminals to court and make sure punishments were carried out.
E. Shire reeve	**v.** The guilt or innocence of a person was decided here.

Knowledge booster

Medieval England

Law enforcement in Norman and later medieval England

8 Complete this table with **at least one** example of continuity (what stayed the same from the period before) and **at least one** example of change for each time period.

	Norman England	Later medieval England
Continuity		
Change		

Punishments in medieval England

9 Define the term **capital punishment**.

....

10 Define the term **corporal punishment**.

....

11 Give **one** example that shows that punishments were often different depending on social status.

....

The influence of the Church

12 Draw lines to match the key terms on the left to the definitions on the right.

A. Benefit of clergy
B. Trial by ordeal
C. Sanctuary

i. If a person could prove they were a member of the clergy, they would be tried in a Church court.
ii. Someone accused of a crime could claim protection from the law in some churches for 40 days.
iii. When someone accused of a crime was tested with something painful or dangerous to decide if they were guilty.

Revision Guide

How did you do? Go to pages 1–6 of the Revision Guide to remind yourself of any points you aren't sure about, and for more about this key topic.

Knowledge booster

Early modern England

This key topic is about crime and punishment in early modern England from c1500 to c1700. It covers the nature and definitions of criminal activity and the nature of law enforcement and punishment in this period.

The nature of crime in early modern England

1 Tick (✓) the statement that best describes changes to crime in early modern England.

A. All types of crime decreased. ☐

B. All types of crime increased. ☐

C. Only crimes against property increased. ☐

D. Crime stayed the same. ☐

2 What was **heresy**?

....

....

'New' crimes in the sixteenth century

3 Decide which statements are true and which are false. Circle your answers.

A.	A vagrant or vagabond was an unemployed, homeless person.	**True**	**False**
B.	Vagabonds were well-liked in England at this time.	**True**	**False**
C.	People believed there were two types of poor, 'deserving' and 'undeserving'.	**True**	**False**
D.	People in early modern England were no longer afraid of witches.	**True**	**False**
E.	In early modern England, witchcraft could be punished by death.	**True**	**False**

Law enforcement in early modern England

4 Give **two** examples of how the role of the Church in law enforcement became less important.

- ....
- ....

5 Which of the following statements best describes the role of local communities in law enforcement? Tick (✓) the correct answer.

A. Local communities were responsible for most law enforcement and provided town watchmen and constables. ☐

B. Local communities had some responsibility for law enforcement, but were supported by a national police force. ☐

C. All law enforcement was handled by a national police force. ☐

Knowledge booster

Early modern England

Punishment in early modern England

6 Give **two** examples of punishments that continued to be used in early modern England.

- ....
- ....

7 Give **one** reason why transportation was introduced as a new punishment.

....

....

The Gunpowder Plotters, 1605

8 Put these events in order. Write numbers in the boxes to show your answer.

☐ **A.** The plotters rented a house near the Houses of Parliament.

☐ **B.** James I came to the throne.

☐ **C.** A group of Catholics plotted to kill James I.

☐ **D.** Guy Fawkes was arrested and tortured.

☐ **E.** Lord Monteagle received a letter.

☐ **F.** James I continued with anti-Catholic laws.

☐ **G.** A cellar, underneath Parliament, was rented and filled with gunpowder.

☐ **H.** The plotters were sentenced to be hanged, drawn and quartered.

The witch-hunts of 1645–47

9 Add **two** more examples to this concept map.

How did the English Civil War intensify the witch-hunts?

- It caused bad harvests – people wanted scapegoats
- It weakened the control of local authorities
- It increased religious differences – Puritans believed Catholics practised witchcraft

10 Give **two** features of Matthew Hopkins' role in the 1645–47 witch-hunts.

- ....
- ....

Revision Guide

How did you do? Go to pages 7–12 of the Revision Guide to remind yourself of any points you aren't sure about, and for more about this key topic.

Knowledge booster

18th- and 19th-century Britain

This key topic is about crime and punishment in Britain from c1700 to c1900. It covers the nature and definitions of criminal activity and the nature of law enforcement and punishment in this period.

Changes in the nature of crime against the person and property

1 Give **one** example of how crimes against property changed in this period.

....

2 Why did highway robbery increase in the eighteenth century? Give **one** reason.

....

....

Crimes against authority: the Tolpuddle Martyrs

3 Decide which statements are true and which are false. Circle your answers.

A.	The Tolpuddle Martyrs were a group of farm workers.	**True**	**False**
B.	They complained that the government would not allow poaching.	**True**	**False**
C.	They were sentenced to death.	**True**	**False**
D.	A petition with 200 000 signatures protested their harsh punishment.	**True**	**False**
E.	The government pardoned them in 1836.	**True**	**False**

Law enforcement in the 18th and 19th centuries

4 Complete the flowchart below to show how law enforcement changed in the 1700s and 1800s.

Before 1700, there was no police force. Towns appointed watchmen.

In the early 1700s, there was continuity in who dealt with crime...

In 1749, Henry Fielding...

In 1829...

In 1856...

18th- and 19th-century Britain

Changing views on the purpose of punishment

5 Complete the sentences below using some of these words: capital; corporal; decreased; equal; increased; rehabilitate.

During the 1800s, more people began to feel that punishments should .... the crime. The use of the death penalty .... as more people believed .... punishment was inhumane except for very serious crimes. The use of transportation and imprisonment therefore ....

6 Name the **two** reformers who worked to improve health and education in prisons.

- ....
- ....

Pentonville Prison

7 Define the term **separate system**.

....

....

8 Give **two** reasons why people in the 1800s supported the design of Pentonville Prison and the idea of the separate system.

- ....
- ....

Robert Peel

9 This concept map gives three main contributions that Robert Peel made to law and order in Britain. For each contribution, add **at least one** example of what Peel changed.

Revision Guide

How did you do? Go to pages 13–18 of the Revision Guide to remind yourself of any points you aren't sure about, and for more about this key topic.

Knowledge booster

Modern Britain

This key topic is about crime and punishment in modern Britain from c1900 to the present day. It covers the nature and definitions of criminal activity, and the nature of law enforcement and punishment in this period.

The nature of crime in modern Britain

1 Tick (✓) the statement which best describes the nature of crime in the twentieth century.

A. Many twentieth-century crimes were completely new. ☐

B. Twentieth-century crimes were mainly new ways of committing older crimes. ☐

C. Terrorism was a completely new crime in the twentieth century. ☐

D. Smuggling was a completely new crime in the twentieth century. ☐

2 Give **one** example of how an older type of crime changed in the twentieth century.

....

Changing definitions of crime in modern Britain

3 Add **two** examples of new crimes to the table. Then add **at least one** detail for each new type of crime.

New crimes	Details
Race crime	New race crimes were defined by the 1968 Race Relations Act and 2006 Racial and Religious Hatred Act.

Law enforcement in modern Britain

4 Decide which statements are true and which are false. Circle your answers.

A.	Police in modern Britain have faster transport than in previous centuries.	**True**	**False**
B.	The police in modern Britain have a unit that tackles online crime.	**True**	**False**
C.	The police in modern Britain do not have armed officers.	**True**	**False**
D.	Neighbourhood Watch groups are teams of professional, local police officers.	**True**	**False**

5 Give **two** examples of technology used by the police in modern Britain.

- ....
- ....

Modern Britain

Changes to punishment in modern Britain

6 Give **two** examples of how prisons have changed since 1900.

- ....
- ....

7 Give **two** examples of punishments that have been used instead of prison since the end of the twentieth century.

- ....
- ....

Treatment of conscientious objectors

8 Define the term **conscientious objector**.

....

9 Draw lines to make three complete statements about the treatment of conscientious objectors (COs) in the First and Second World Wars.

A. In the two World Wars, the treatment of COs by the government...	**i.** ...was very similar.
B. In the two World Wars, the treatment of COs by the general public...	**ii.** ...were cowards and traitors.
C. Many members of the public thought that COs...	**iii.** ...was very different.

The Derek Bentley case, 1953

10 Give **one** reason why some people felt that Bentley did not deserve the death penalty.

....

11 Give **two** ways in which the Derek Bentley case was significant for the abolition of the death penalty.

- ....
  ....
- ....
  ....

Revision Guide

How did you do? Go to pages 19–24 of the Revision Guide to remind yourself of any points you aren't sure about, and for more about this key topic.

Knowledge booster

Whitechapel, c1870–c1900

The historic environment for this thematic study is Whitechapel, c1870–c1900. It covers crime, policing and the inner city.

The Metropolitan Police

1 Decide which statements are true and which are false. Circle your answers.

A.	There were problems with police constables drinking on the job.	**True**	**False**
B.	Beat constables were policemen who detected crimes.	**True**	**False**
C.	Sir Charles Warren was appointed Met Commissioner in 1886.	**True**	**False**
D.	The police answered to the Prime Minister.	**True**	**False**
E.	The police were popular with the working-classes in London.	**True**	**False**

The local context of Whitechapel

2 Complete the concept map by adding **at least five** examples of why Whitechapel had a high crime rate.

Tensions in Whitechapel

3 Fill in the gaps to complete this description of tensions in Whitechapel. Use some of these words: permanent; lodging; temporary; community.

In Whitechapel, a large part of the population lived in .... accommodation. A common place to stay was in .... houses. Because people moved a lot, there was no sense of ....

4 Give **two** examples of why immigration caused tensions in Whitechapel to rise.

- ....
- ....

Knowledge booster

Whitechapel, c1870–c1900

The organisation of policing in Whitechapel

5 These are problems that H Division faced in policing Whitechapel. Rank them from most challenging (1) to least challenging (7). Write numbers in the boxes to show your answer. Make sure you can give reasons for your choice.

- ☐ **A.** The environment
- ☐ **B.** Gangs
- ☐ **C.** Violent demonstrations
- ☐ **D.** Prostitution
- ☐ **E.** Alcohol
- ☐ **F.** Protection rackets
- ☐ **G.** Attacks on Jews

Investigative policing in Whitechapel

6 Complete the concept map with **at least three** examples of techniques of detective investigation used by the police in the 1880s.

Police techniques

- Searching houses, pubs and opium dens

7 Give **two** reasons why investigative policing improved after 1888.

- ....
- ....

Dealing with the crimes of Jack the Ripper

8 Give **two** examples of how the media made investigating the Ripper murders more challenging.

- ....
- ....

9 The media was not the only reason the police failed to solve the Ripper murders. Give **one** other reason.

....

....

Revision Guide

How did you do? Go to pages 25–29 of the Revision Guide to remind yourself of any points you aren't sure about, and for more about this key topic.

In the exam

After all your revision and preparation, you want to do well. There are some key things you should remember in the exam.

What should I take with me?

- You must write in **black**, so it is a good idea to have more than one black pen with you.
- You might want a highlighter to mark the key words in the questions.
- Don't fill your desk with loads of other things – you know you won't need a calculator, for example, so leave it in your bag.
- Don't bother with correction fluid – just cross out any mistakes.

Where should I start?

Start with the front cover of your exam paper.

- The most important bit is the space for your name – don't forget to write it!
- It tells you how much time you have for the exam.
- For Paper 1, it will remind you about the separate Sources Booklet – make sure you have this.
- It will tell you which questions you must answer, and which ones you can choose.

How can I stay focused?

1. Take deep, slow breaths at the start of the exam and to help you to focus as you work through the paper.
2. Highlight the key words in the questions, like dates, to make sure you focus on the right thing.
3. Plan your answers, especially for the longer essay questions. Work out what you want to say before you start writing.
4. If you get stuck, try a new question and come back to the other one later. Or make a list of what you do know about the topic in the question to help you get started.

How can I manage my time?

- It is a good idea to divide your time. Spend more time on questions that are worth more marks. You could even write on the paper (on the front cover or next to each question) the time you will start each question before you begin answering.
- Check the time regularly to make sure that you still have enough time for the longer answers.
- If you haven't finished answering a low-mark question but you are running out of time, move on to a higher-mark question. You can come back if you need to.

How much should I write?

- Your exam paper will give you space to write in for each question.
- Use the number of marks as a guide to how much you should write – a 12-mark question will need more than a 4-mark one.
- You don't always need to fill the space – this does not necessarily mean more marks.

How should I check my work?

Top tip

- Leave about five minutes at the end for checking.
- Check that you didn't miss any questions.
- Check your spelling and punctuation.
- Check that you have not made any obvious mistakes, like using the wrong date.

If you run out of space to finish an answer, **ask for more paper**. Don't use the answer space for the next question – this will make your answer hard to read. If you use extra paper, write 'answer on extra paper' at the bottom of the answer space. Then write the question number on the extra paper and complete your answer. At the end, check any extra paper has your name on it and that it is clear which answers you have finished there.

Had a look ☐ Nearly there ☐ Nailed it! ☐

Writing clear answers

The most important thing in the exam is writing down the correct information, but it also helps to write clear, well-organised answers. This will make your answers easier to follow.

Get the basics right

- ✓ Use a good, **black** pen.
- ✓ Use paragraphs – they will help to make your points clearer.
- ✓ Write in the correct answer spaces. If you use extra paper, add a label to the new page to make it clear which question you are continuing. Write 'answer on extra paper' where you ran out of space.
- ✓ If you make a mistake, cross it out neatly.

How can I write clearly?

1. Always write in Standard English – formal language, not slang.
2. Use adverbials or linking phrases to connect ideas and make your meaning clear – such as, 'for example', 'however', 'therefore', 'as a result', 'consequently', 'in addition', 'significantly', 'in contrast', 'similarly'.
3. Use key terms for the topic.

Does my handwriting matter?

Your work will be marked, no matter what your handwriting is like. **However**, it is always a good idea to write as neatly as you can to make sure all the words in your answer are clear.

Imagine you had to mark these sentences. Which is easiest to read?

One reason for this is

Should I plan my answers?

Top tip

Plans help you to organise your ideas.

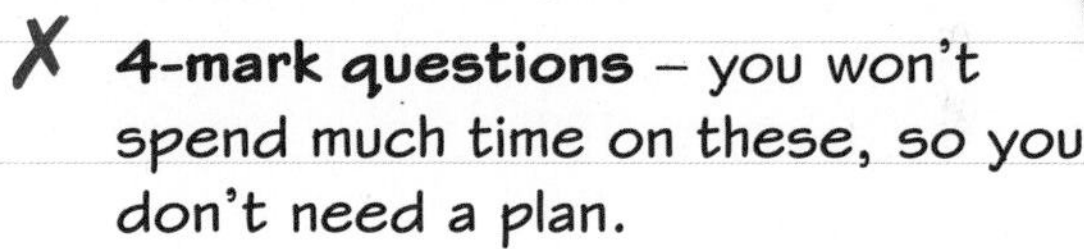

- ✗ **4-mark questions** – you won't spend much time on these, so you don't need a plan.
- ✓ **8-mark questions** – you might find it helpful to jot down a quick plan, such as a short list of points to include.
- ✓ **12-mark and 16-mark questions** – make a plan for these questions. Many of the best exam answers for these questions have plans.

There are different ways to plan. You can see examples on pages 25, 37 and 41, and in the answers to the practice paper.

How can I write effective paragraphs?

A good way to write effective paragraphs is to use **PEEL – Point, Evidence, Explain, Link:**

POINT – say what the paragraph is about.

EVIDENCE – give examples.

EXPLAIN – say what the evidence shows.

LINK – connect back to the question. This paragraph is answering the question 'Explain why punishments changed in the years 1700–1900'.

One reason that punishments changed in the 1800s was that they were not effective. In the 1700s and 1800s, juries did not like finding people guilty because they did not like sentencing them to death. Only a small number of criminals found guilty were hanged. It was clear to the government that this was not an effective way of stopping crime. As a result, transportation and fines became more common instead. This meant that the type of punishments changed.

Had a look ☐ **Nearly there** ☐ **Nailed it!** ☐

Working with sources

You need to know how to look at sources and how to work with them in the exam.

What is a source?

A source is a piece of historical evidence from the time period you are looking at.

When you read or examine a source, look for three things:

- What is the source about?
- Is there an opinion or a message in the source?
- Does the source agree with or challenge what you know about the topic?

What sources are in the exam?

- There will be two sources. You will find them in a separate Sources Booklet.
- At least one of the sources will be a written source (like a diary entry or a speech). The other could be a written source or an image (like a poster or a photograph).
- They will be connected to your study of the historic environment, Whitechapel, c1870–c1900: crime, policing and the inner city.

Analysing the content of a source

Source A: From a newspaper article describing what a journalist saw as he walked through Whitechapel, published in the *Daily News*, November 1888.

> Whitechapel shows the dreadful possibilities of life. A visitor can see here and there a glimpse of faces in the gloom, bloated by drink. Some streets are deserted after nightfall. Turn down a side street. It may be well to tuck out of view any bit of jewellery that may be glittering. The street is oppressively dark. Men are lounging at the doors of the shops, smoking evil-smelling pipes. Women are sauntering about in twos and threes, or are seated gossiping on steps leading into passages dark as night. Now round the corner into another still gloomier passage. This is the notorious Wentworth Street. The police used to make a point of going through this only in pairs, but now they rarely go down there.

About: the poor conditions of life in Whitechapel.

Agrees with what I know: alcohol was a serious problem in Whitechapel.

Message: Whitechapel is a gloomy, threatening place full of winding narrow streets.

Source B: An engraving published in a guidebook to London called *London, a Pilgrimage* in 1872. It is called 'Waifs and Strays' and shows homeless and unemployed people.

Message: there were many homeless and unemployed, including men, women and children.

Agrees with what I know: many residents needed to beg or get enough work to pay for a night in a doss-house or end up on the street.

About: the problem of homelessness and unemployment in Whitechapel.

Annotate or highlight key points in the sources as you read or look at them. This will help you to find ideas to include in your answer.

Had a look ☐ Nearly there ☐ Nailed it! ☐

Working with sources

How can I spot a message in a source?

1. Look at the words that have been chosen. Are they positive (like 'victory' or 'success') or negative (like 'disaster' or 'failure')?
2. Does the source exaggerate anything? Does it only give examples from one point of view?
3. In illustrations, has the artist made anyone look smart and intelligent, or stupid and ridiculous?

Most sources were not made just to share information. They were designed with a purpose. This could be to share an opinion, to persuade others that something is good or bad, or to make people support something. A historian needs to learn to spot the message and the purpose.

In Paper 1, you will be asked about sources in Question 2a (which is about the usefulness of a source) and Question 2b (which asks how you would follow up a source). You can find more about these questions on pages 23–30.

Provenance: nature, origin and purpose

The **provenance** of a source is its **nature**, **origin** and **purpose**.

Nature	What type of source is it?	For example, is it a newspaper article, speech, leaflet, letter, diary entry, book, postcard, poster, cartoon or photograph?
Origin	Where is it from?	Who wrote it? Were they involved with the event? Is it from before, after or during the event? Is it from where the events happened or from somewhere else?
Purpose	Why was it made?	Was it made to inform people? Persuade people? Sell something? Give evidence to make a decision? Was it made for the public or for a specific person or group of people?

Identifying the nature, origin and purpose (NOP) of a source is an important skill. It will help you to judge whether a source is likely to be reliable, balanced or accurate. For Paper 1, you will need this skill for Question 2a.

Where can I find the provenance?

Start by looking at the key information about provenance that comes just before the source itself. This can give you a lot of information:

- what the source is
- who made or wrote it
- when they made or wrote it.

Top tip

Always read the key information about provenance first. The source itself may have information about NOP too, but starting with the key information will help you to spot words or details in the source which show the opinion or message of the person who created it.

The source is part of a newspaper article.

Source A: From a newspaper article describing what a journalist saw as he walked through Whitechapel, published in the *Daily News*, November 1888.

It was published in November 1888, shortly after the Ripper murders had happened.

It was written by a journalist. He will have made his living writing stories that seem exciting.

Had a look ☐ Nearly there ☐ Nailed it! ☐

Using key terms

Using key terms helps to show you know and understand the topic.

What key terms might I need to use?

abolition – ending something, like a law
capital punishment – punishing a criminal by killing them
civil war – a war between people in the same country, like the English Civil War of 1642–51
conscientious objectors – people who refuse to fight due to their beliefs
constable – a person whose job it is to enforce the law (the exact role has changed over time)
corporal punishment – punishing a criminal by physically hurting them
custodial – if a sentence is custodial it means the criminal is put in prison
deterrence – discouraging people from committing crime through fear of the consequences
heresy – the crime of having religious beliefs different from the official beliefs of a religion
highway robbery – robbing travellers by threatening or attacking them
hue and cry – the medieval way of getting people to chase criminals
martyr – someone who is killed for their beliefs
metropolitan – a city area, like London
Neighbourhood Watch – a group of volunteers who look out for criminals in the area where they live
ordeal – a medieval trial to find out who was guilty
parish – the area a local priest looks after
penal – laws for punishing criminals
poaching – hunting on private land
prosecution – taking a person to court for a crime
reform – changing something, often an institution or law
retribution – making a criminal suffer for the crime they committed
sanctuary – protection from punishment in a church
separate and silent system – keeping prisoners apart from each other and not allowing talking
smuggling – bringing items into or out of the country illegally
tithings – groups of ten men (if one committed a crime, all were held responsible)
treason – committing crimes against the country
Wergild – money medieval people paid as compensation for a crime
transportation – punishing a criminal by shipping them to another country
vagabond – a person who was homeless and wandered from place to place, begging

Make sure that you can spell foreign or very old words, like **Wergild**, correctly.

The key terms with capital letters will always use capital letters, wherever they appear in a sentence.

The key terms on this page are the most important ones. If you think of others, write them down in the back of this book.

What about dates?

Make sure you can write about dates and time periods accurately. For example:

✓ The year **1560** was in the **16th century**.
✓ The **1700s** were the **18th century**.

A century is a period of 100 years. To find the century, knock the last two digits off the year and add one. For example:

1759 → 17 + 1 = 18 → 18th century

Remember: 'c' before a year means 'around' – for example, 'c1700' means 'around 1700'.

Had a look ☐ **Nearly there** ☐ **Nailed it!** ☐

SPaG

Good spelling, punctuation and grammar (SPaG) are important in every exam, but in your Paper 1 exam four marks are available specifically for SPaG and your use of specialist terminology.

What are the SPaG marks for?

For Paper 1, SPaG is tested on Question 5/6.

You can get up to four marks for your quality of written communication.

The best responses:

- ✓ have accurate spelling and punctuation throughout the answer
- ✓ use the rules of grammar to write clearly throughout the answer
- ✓ use a wide range of key terms.

What about key terms?

Use key terms to show your topic knowledge, like 'smuggling' in the stronger example below.

✗ In the 1700s, a common crime was bringing things into the country illegally.

✓ In the 1700s, a common crime was smuggling.

Tricky words

Some important words are often spelled incorrectly. Make sure you can spell these words:

appearance	beginning	benefited
exaggerate	government	monarch
occurred	Parliament	purpose
preparation	professional	soldier

When you find other tricky words, list them at the back of this book.

Formal language

Use…	✓	✗
Standard English, not slang	police	cops
Correct grammar	would have	would of

Use homophones (words that sound the same but have different meanings) correctly. For example, make sure you know whether to use 'their' or 'there'.

Writing clear sentences

Sentences that are clear start with capital letters, end with full-stops and are not too long.

✗ From about 1740 more people began to smuggle goods because import taxes were so high that it was cheaper to smuggle goods into the country and the government found it hard to stop this type of crime.

✓ From about 1740 more people began to smuggle goods. This was because import taxes were so high that it was cheaper to smuggle goods. The government found it hard to stop this type of crime.

The second example, with shorter sentences, is easier to read.

Punctuation for meaning

Use punctuation to make your meaning clear:

- Use commas to separate ideas or information.
- Use commas between items in a list.
- Use apostrophes to show that something belongs to something else.

✓ The police chased the criminals, using cars and helicopters. The policeman's radio allowed him to keep in touch with other officers.

The comma shows that the police were using the cars and helicopters, not the criminals.

The apostrophe shows that the radio belonged to the policeman.

Had a look ☐ Nearly there ☐ Nailed it! ☐

Understanding your exam

It is a good idea to understand how your exam paper works. You will know what to expect and this will help you to feel confident when you are in the exam.

Paper 1 thematic study and historic environment

Your thematic study is your Paper 1 exam. Paper 1 is...

 a written exam

 1 hour 15 minutes

 worth 52 marks

% worth 30% of your GCSE History.

What will I get in the exam?

- You will get an exam paper. The paper has spaces to write your answers in.
- You will also get a Sources Booklet. This will contain two sources which you will need to use to answer the questions in Section A of the exam paper.

Section A is on the historic environment and Section B is on the thematic study.

What is a thematic study and what is a historic environment?

This paper – Crime and punishment in Britain, c1000–present – explores a long period of British history, about 1000 years in length. It is called a thematic study because, instead of focusing on one specific period, you will look at themes through the period, exploring what changes and what stays the same. As part of the topic, you will study a historic environment – a case study of a location during a specific period of time. In this case, the historic environment is Whitechapel, 1870–1900: crime, policing and the inner city.

What historical skills does Paper 1 assess?

Your GCSE History exam papers are designed to assess different historical skills, or 'Assessment Objectives' (AOs).

Your Paper 1 thematic study and historic environment will assess these assessment objectives:

AO1 – Demonstrate knowledge and understanding of the key features of the period.

This means you need to show your knowledge of the topic, including details of the main events, people and themes.

AO2 – Explain and analyse events using second-order historical concepts.

This means you need to analyse historical ideas in your answers – these ideas are called **second-order historical concepts**.

The second-order historical concepts are: causation (why things happened), consequences (the results of something), similarity, difference, change, continuity (staying the same) and significance (how important an event, idea or change was).

AO3 – Analyse, evaluate and use sources to make substantiated judgements.

This means you need to use historical sources to investigate a topic, and make judgements about how useful they are.

You can find out more about working with sources on pages 13–14.

Substantiated means backing something up. A substantiated judgement is a judgement which is supported with a reason.

Had a look ☐ **Nearly there** ☐ **Nailed it!** ☐

Understanding your exam

What type of questions will be on the exam paper for Paper 1?

The questions for Paper 1 will always follow the same pattern:

SECTION A: Historic environment

1 Describe **two** features of...

(4 marks)

Question 1 is the **describing** question:
- (4) Worth 4 marks
- Tests AO1
- Spend about 5 minutes
- Describe **two** different features of the topic.

2a Study Sources A and B.

How useful are Sources A and B for an enquiry into...?

(8 marks)

Question 2a is the **assessing usefulness** question:
- (8) Worth 8 marks
- Tests AO3
- Spend about 14 minutes
- Use both sources and your own knowledge.

2b Study Source A/B.

How could you follow up Source A/B to find out more about...?

(4 marks)

Question 2b is the **follow-up enquiry** question:
- (4) Worth 4 marks
- Tests AO3
-  Spend about 5 minutes
-  Show how you would continue an enquiry.

SECTION B: Thematic study

3 Explain **one** way in which... was/were similar/different...

(4 marks)

Question 3 is the **making comparisons** question:
- (4) Worth 4 marks
-  Tests AO1 and AO2
-  Spend about 5 minutes
-  Explain **one** similarity or difference.

4 Explain why...

(12 marks)

Question 4 is the **explaining why** question:
- (12) Worth 12 marks
-  Tests AO1 and AO2
-  Spend about 18 minutes
- You must use some of your own information.

5/6 'A statement.'

How far do you agree?

(16 marks plus 4 marks for SPaG and use of specialist terminology)

Question 5/6 is the **judgement** question:
- (16) + (4) Worth 16 marks, plus 4 for SPaG
-  Tests AO1 and AO2
-  Spend about 25 minutes
- You need to reach a judgement.

Had a look ☐  **Nearly there** ☐ **Nailed it!** ☐

Understanding Question 1

Question 1 will always be structured in the same way. Make sure you know how this question works and what it is asking you to do.

How does Question 1 work?

This tells you that you need to write about **two** separate features.

Identify the command word – this question will always ask you to 'describe'.

1 Describe **two** features of the Whitechapel Vigilance Committee.

(4 marks)

This is the topic for the question. The two features you describe must be linked to this topic.

Check how many marks the question is worth – this will help you to manage your time.

Links This question is similar to Question 1a on Paper 2 (your British depth study).

What does Question 1 assess?

- Question 1 tests Assessment Objective 1.
- You need to show your knowledge of the topic.
- This will involve giving details of features related to the historic environment – Whitechapel, 1870–1900: crime, policing and the inner city.

How long should I spend?

Spend about 5 minutes on Question 1.

Try not to spend longer than this as the next questions will need plenty of time.

Take a look at page 17 for more about the assessment objectives.

What does 'describe' mean?

Describe means that your answer should show that you understand what the topic in the question is. You don't need to give reasons for it, or say how important it was. You just need to give two separate pieces of information about the topic.

Top tip

The key thing to remember is that you can pick any two features but they **must** be connected to the topic in the question.

What is a 'feature'?

A **feature** is a relevant piece of information about the topic. This could be what happened, who was involved, how it affected people or any other detail about the topic. For example, with the question above about the Whitechapel Vigilance Committee, you could mention:

- who they were
- what they did
- the effect they had
- any other relevant features.

Had a look ☐ **Nearly there** ☐ **Nailed it!** ☐

Understanding Question 1

Features and supporting information

Each feature you describe in your answer needs supporting information. This means you need to add a bit more detail to each feature you identify. For example, for the question on the Whitechapel Vigilance Committee on page 19, you could have this feature and supporting information:

One feature was that the committee disrupted the police investigation into the Ripper murders.

This is a **valid feature** of the Whitechapel Vigilance Committee. This would get one mark.

They did this by encouraging criticism of the police investigation in the media.

This is **supporting information** that adds to the feature about the Whitechapel Vigilance Committee. It is not a new feature. This would get one mark.

How is Question 1 marked?

Marks are available for identifying the features and for providing supporting information:

- There is **one mark available for each valid feature** you identify – so one mark for giving one feature, and two marks for giving two features. Adding more features does not improve your mark.
- There is **one mark available** for adding supporting information to one of your features, and **two marks** if you add supporting information to both of your features.

Using language to write clear answers

To make your answer clear, you could introduce each feature like this:

One feature was…

A second feature was…

Remember to use **key terms** in your answer.

Turn to page 12 for more about writing clear answers. You can find examples of key terms on page 15.

Top tips for success

Top tip

- ✓ Describe **two different features** – take care not to use the same feature twice.
- ✓ Use **valid** features – make sure that both features are connected to the topic in the question.
- ✓ For each feature, write two sentences – one to **identify** the feature and one to add **supporting information** that is connected to that feature.
- ✓ Keep your answers **concise** – don't write more than you need to.
- ✓ **Use the space** on the exam paper – there will be a space marked for each feature.
- ✓ Be specific – avoid very general, vague sentences (like 'the Whitechapel Vigilance Committee was important').
- ✓ Be accurate – use correct facts to support your features.

Had a look ☐ Nearly there ☐ Nailed it! ☐

Answering Question 1

You need to understand how you can write a successful answer to Question 1.

Reading the question

Always read the question carefully before you start writing your answer. Make sure you are clear about what the topic of the question is.

1 Describe **two** features of the Whitechapel Vigilance Committee.

(4 marks)

Short, 4-mark questions do not need a plan.

Steps to success

1 Identify **one** valid feature of the topic. Write **one** sentence about it.

Feature 1

One feature was that it was set up by businessmen in Whitechapel.

Answer in the correct space on the page. Describe your first feature in the space for 'Feature 1'.

Identify one valid feature which is relevant to the topic.

2 **Add information** to support your first feature, using your knowledge of the topic. Write **one** sentence.

They were frustrated that the police were failing to catch Jack the Ripper.

Add a sentence of supporting information.

Make sure the supporting information is connected to your first feature – it should not be an unconnected fact.

3 Identify a **second** valid feature of the topic. Write **one** sentence about it.

Feature 2

A second feature was that members of the Committee patrolled the streets of Whitechapel at night.

Identify a second feature which is relevant to the topic.

Make sure your second feature is different to your first feature.

4 **Add information** to support your second feature, using your knowledge of the topic. Write **one** sentence.

They carried torches to light the dark alleys and whistles to call for help.

Add a sentence of supporting information.

Make sure the supporting information is connected to your second feature.

Had a look ☐ **Nearly there** ☐ **Nailed it!** ☐

Answering Question 1

Getting it right

Question 1 should be a good chance to get some straightforward marks at the beginning of your exam paper. Stay focused on the question and don't write more than you need to. Look at these examples.

Feature 1

One feature was that members of the Committee aimed to catch the Ripper in the act. **(1)** They did this by wearing noisy hob-nail boots on their patrols. **(1)**

Feature 2

A second feature was that the Committee patrolled the streets as loudly as possible to stop the Ripper in his tracks.

✓ The first feature is valid – the Committee did hope to catch the Ripper. It also has relevant supporting information, which is an example of how they tried to do this. So, Feature 1 would get 2 marks.

✗ The second feature repeats the first feature, so does not get any marks. To improve, this answer needs a second feature that is different to the first one.

Feature 1

One feature was that some of the members just wanted to make the police look stupid. **(1)** They also wanted to embarrass the government.

Feature 2

A second feature was that the Committee patrolled the streets every night. **(1)** The reward was for information leading to the capture of the murderer.

✓ This is a valid feature.

✗ This supporting information is not connected to the feature so does not get any marks. The supporting information should be about how they made the police look stupid.

✓ This is also a valid feature.

✗ Again the supporting information is not connected to the feature so does not get a mark. It should be about the nightly patrols by the Committee.

Feature 1

One feature was that the Committee was formed on 10 September 1888. **(1)** This was shortly after the second Ripper murder victim was found. **(1)**

Feature 2

A second feature was that the Committee offered rewards for any information about the Ripper. **(1)** This led to many false leads from people trying to claim the reward. **(1)**

✓ This is a valid feature. It also has supporting information that develops the feature. So, Feature 1 would get 2 marks.

✓ This is a second, different feature, which also has supporting information. So, Feature 2 would get 2 marks.

Did you notice that the features in this strong answer are different to the ones in the answer on page 21? It doesn't matter which features you describe as long as they are accurate and valid.

Had a look ☐ Nearly there ☐ Nailed it! ☐

Understanding Question 2a

Question 2a will always be structured in the same way. Make sure you know how this question works and what it is asking you to do.

How does Question 2a work?

In the exam, Sources A and B will be in a Sources Booklet. For this question, you will find Sources A and B on page 13.

Identify the command phrase – this question will always ask you to consider 'how useful' the sources are for a particular enquiry.

2a Study Sources A and B on page 13.

How useful are Sources A and B for an enquiry into the conditions in Whitechapel that encouraged crime?

Explain your answer, using Sources A and B and your knowledge of the historical context.

(8 marks)

This is the **enquiry** (area of investigation) you need to focus on.

You must refer to both sources and use your own knowledge.

Check how many marks the question is worth – this will help you to manage your time.

This question is similar to Question 3a on Paper 3 (your modern depth study).

What does Question 2a assess?

- Question 2a tests Assessment Objective 3.
- You need to use historical sources to investigate a topic.
- You need to make judgements about how useful the sources are for the enquiry given in the question.

How long should I spend?

Spend about 14 minutes on Question 2a.

Remember that you need to look at **both** sources. Divide your time equally between them so you give them equal attention in your answer.

Take a look at page 17 for more about the assessment objectives.

Why do I need to focus on the enquiry in the question?

Top tip

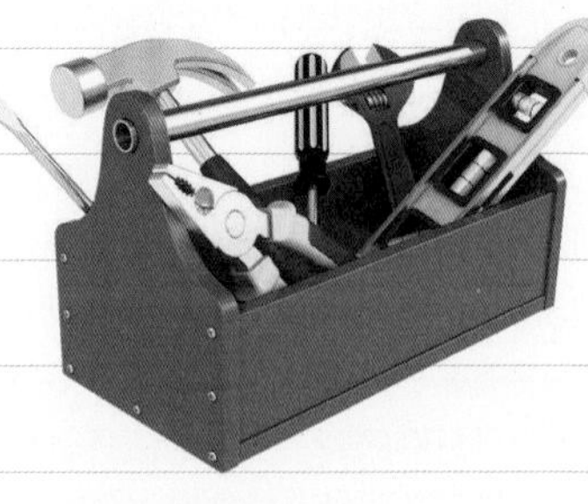

Imagine a toolbox. It has different tools, such as hammers, screwdrivers and saws. Each tool is useful in one way or another. But **how** useful each tool is depends on the job you need to do. For example, if you need to hit a nail into a wall, a hammer is useful, whereas a saw is not – but if you need to cut a piece of wood, the saw is a very useful tool.

All sources are useful in some ways, but depending on the enquiry topic, their usefulness will change. For example, look at Source B on page 13. It is very useful for investigating some enquiries, like the conditions in Whitechapel that encouraged crime, but less useful for studying solutions to the problem of poverty. So, **when you consider how useful the sources are for Question 2a, make sure you stay focused on the enquiry in the question.**

Had a look ☐ **Nearly there** ☐ **Nailed it!** 

Understanding Question 2a

How to judge usefulness

To judge **usefulness** you need to assess how useful the source is for the enquiry in the question.

To measure usefulness, you need to think about two things:

- ✓ How much can you learn about the enquiry topic from the source's content?
- ✓ Is the source giving you accurate information?

What's in the source?

Pick out points from the content of the source which give information about the enquiry topic. If the source contains information that is relevant then it is useful for the enquiry.

Compare the content to your own knowledge. If the source supports what you know about the topic, it is more useful.

Remember: Focus on what **is** in the source, not on what is missing. Missing content is only important if it should be in the source but isn't.

Is the information accurate?

You need to consider whether the information in the source is accurate:

- Is it balanced? For example, a balanced, confidential account written for a government department making policies might be likely to contain accurate details.
- Or is it presenting the information in a one-sided or exaggerated way? For example, a newspaper cartoon which is criticising a politician might be exaggerated.

Generally, a source which is more accurate and more balanced will be more useful than one that is exaggerated and one-sided. However, if the enquiry is about people's opinions, sometimes a one-sided, exaggerated source is more useful for showing what people thought.

Look at the **provenance – nature, origin and purpose** – of the source. Does this make the source more or less useful?

You can find more about nature, origin and purpose on page 14.

Remember: A source can be useful even if it is unreliable. For example, Source A on page 13 is less reliable as the author is probably exaggerating the gloom and danger to make his account more exciting to his readers, but if we are studying the conditions in Whitechapel that encouraged crime, Source A is still useful because it shows that the dark alleys of Whitechapel were dangerous places.

How is Question 2a marked?

Strong answers to Question 2a:

- ✓ judge the usefulness of each source for the enquiry given in the question
- ✓ explain clearly how the provenance of each source makes it more or less useful
- ✓ support their judgements with comments on each source's content and provenance
- ✓ use own knowledge to interpret the sources and support their judgements.

You don't need to compare the sources and you don't need to decide which one is more useful. Write about one source, then the other – without comparing them.

Top tips for success

Top tip

- ✓ Stay focused on the enquiry given in the question – **decide how useful each source is for this enquiry.**
- ✓ Refer to **both sources** in your answer – make a judgement about the usefulness of each one.
- ✓ Analyse the **content** and **provenance** of each source – **explain why** this makes the source more or less useful.
- ✓ Use **your own knowledge of the topic** to judge the source – does it agree with what you know?
- ✓ Make a **quick plan** before you write to help you to stay focused.

Had a look ☐ Nearly there ☐ Nailed it! ☐

Answering Question 2a

You need to understand how you can write a successful answer to Question 2a.

Reading the question

> **2a Study Sources A and B on page 13.**
>
> How useful are Sources A and B for an enquiry into the conditions in Whitechapel that encouraged crime?
>
> Explain your answer, using Sources A and B and your knowledge of the historical context.
>
> **(8 marks)**

Always read the question carefully before you start writing your answer.

Make sure you are clear about what the enquiry topic of the question is.

Top tip

Remember: No source in the exam will ever be useless for the enquiry. You can say it is not very useful but don't say it is useless.

Writing about usefulness

Use phrases such as 'quite useful', 'very useful' and 'partially useful' to give a clear judgement about the usefulness of a source.

How can I structure my answer?

1. Explain how useful the content of **Source A** is for the enquiry. Use at least one example from the source.
2. Explain how the provenance affects the usefulness of **Source A**. Finish with an overall judgement about usefulness.
3. Repeat Steps 1 and 2 for **Source B**.

Top tip

Remember that you don't need to compare the sources.

You can find more about nature, origin and purpose on page 14.

Plan your answer

This question is worth 8 marks, so note down a quick plan before you start writing.

Source A	Source B
• Dangerous streets, alcohol, overcrowding • Police were assaulted in Whitechapel • Exaggerates to sell, uses Ripper excitement • Quite useful	• Begging and homelessness • Shows changing population • Purpose = to guide, needs accuracy • Not very useful

The best answers are well-organised. Structure your plan clearly to keep your answer focused.

Keep it short. You don't need to write in full sentences.

Include your own knowledge.

You only need one point on NOP – often 'purpose' is the most helpful.

Include a quick judgement about each source.

This is one style of plan. You can see another style on page 64.

Had a look ☐ **Nearly there** ☐ **Nailed it!** ☐

Answering Question 2a

Steps to success

1 Explain how useful the content of **Source A** is for the enquiry topic in the question.

Source A is quite useful for an enquiry into the conditions in Whitechapel that encouraged crime. It describes the 'oppressively' dark alleyways. This agrees with my knowledge, as one reason crime was more likely in Whitechapel was the dark alleys and rookeries, which were ideal places to rob people. It was especially dangerous away from the main streets, which is what the source describes. It also says that there were some streets where the police 'rarely go down'. This was because they were so dangerous that gangs would attack police officers if they went there. The lack of policing was another reason that there was so much crime.

- Start with a quick judgement about the source. This will help you to focus on usefulness.
- Pick out points from the content of the source which give information about the enquiry topic. If the source is a text, like this one, you could include short, relevant quotations.
- Use your own knowledge about the topic to explain how the content of the source fits with the enquiry topic.
- Use key terms to show your knowledge of the topic.
- Explain how your points are linked to the enquiry topic. Use the word 'because' to show you are explaining.
- Focus on a few key points only – you won't have time to cover every detail.

2 Go on to explain how the provenance affects the usefulness of **Source A** for the enquiry topic in the question.

Source A is probably exaggerating the conditions because the journalist wants to excite his readers to sell more copies. He uses words like 'notorious' to make it more interesting to his readers. He probably wanted to use the recent media excitement about the Ripper murders in September 1888 to gain interest in his story. However, this is still useful because the fact he has written the article shows that readers wanted to read about the conditions which encouraged crime in Whitechapel. Source A is overall quite useful for this enquiry because it gives a detailed description of the Whitechapel area which people of the time believed to be true.

- Use NOP to help you decide whether the source is balanced or one-sided – this answer uses the purpose of the source.
- Use the date of the source. How does it fit into the topic and affect the source's usefulness?
- Explain whether the source is balanced and accurate (or not) and why. Remember: balanced, accurate sources are more reliable.
- Explain how the source's reliability affects its usefulness.
- Finish your analysis of Source A with an overall judgement about its usefulness.
- Give a clear reason for your judgement and link it back to the enquiry topic.

3 Repeat Steps 1 and 2 for **Source B**. Explain how useful the content of **Source B** is for the enquiry topic, then explain how the provenance affects its usefulness for the enquiry topic. Remember to finish with an overall judgement about **Source B**'s usefulness.

Had a look ☐ **Nearly there** ☐ **Nailed it!** ☐

Understanding Question 2b

Question 2b will always be structured in the same way. Make sure you know how this question works and what it is asking you to do.

How does Question 2b work?

Identify the source you need to focus on – this question will ask about **either** Source A **or** Source B.

This question will always ask **how** you could **follow up** the source.

> **2b** Study Source A on page 13.
>
> How could you follow up Source A to find out more about the conditions in Whitechapel that encouraged crime?
>
> In your answer, you must give the question you would ask and the type of source you could use.
>
> Complete the table below
>
> **(4 marks)**

This is the enquiry you need to focus on. The enquiry will always be the same as the enquiry in Question 2a.

Check how many marks the question is worth – this will help you to manage your time.

This question gives you a table to complete – you should use this to structure your answer.

What does Question 2b assess?

- Question 2b tests Assessment Objective 3.
- You need to show that you can form questions to carry out a historical enquiry.
- You need to show that you understand the types of sources that a historian might use to investigate a historical enquiry.

How long should I spend?

Spend about 5 minutes on Question 2b.

Try not to spend longer than this as the next questions will need plenty of time.

Take a look at page 17 for more about the assessment objectives.

What does 'follow up' mean?

Follow up means that you need to design a question which a historian could use to find out more about something they have learned from the source. This includes identifying where they could go to find the answer.

Top tip

You must stay focused on the enquiry in the question. This is especially important when you design your follow-up question.

What are the parts of the answer?

1. Identify a **detail** in the source to follow up.
2. Give a **follow-up question** you would ask about the detail you have identified.
3. Suggest a **type of source** you could use to answer your follow-up question.
4. Explain **how** this type of source would help you to answer your follow-up question.

Had a look ☐ Nearly there ☐ Nailed it! ☐

Understanding Question 2b

Identifying a detail in the source

You can pick any detail from the source but:

- The detail **must** be relevant to the enquiry in the question.
- You must identify a **specific** detail – so avoid making general comments.
- The detail must be **from the source itself**, and not from the information about provenance.

Top tip

Make sure you give a detail rather than writing a question for this part of the answer. Quoting a phrase from the source is a good way to do this if the source is a text.

Forming a question

Your follow-up question **must** be:

- linked to the enquiry in the question
- linked to the detail you have already identified in the source.

Your question should be one you could find the answer to and that would help you to understand the enquiry better. For example, you could ask about:

- the reason for the detail
- the consequence of the detail
- whether the detail happened a lot.

Suggesting a type of source

The type of source you choose must help to answer your follow-up question and must be **specific**. These are examples of specific sources:

✓ notebook from a beat constable's patrol during the Ripper murders

✓ records of meetings between the Home Secretary and Police Commissioner

✓ H Division employment records of police officers.

Avoid vague general sources like these:

✗ police records

✗ diaries from someone at the time.

Explaining how the source will help

You need to explain how the type of source you have identified could help to answer your follow-up question. What sort of information would the source contain? How could you use this?

Make sure your explanation is precise:

✓ I would be able to see how many crimes occurred in quieter side streets or on busier main roads.

Avoid giving an explanation that is too general:

✗ It would tell me what I want to know.

How is Question 2b marked?

There is **one mark available for each part of the question**. This means:

✓ one mark for identifying a valid detail in the source

✓ one mark for a follow-up question linked to the detail chosen

✓ one mark for a type of source that could be used to answer the follow-up question

✓ one mark for an explanation of how the source could help to answer the follow-up question.

The parts of your answer must link together.

Top tips for success

Top tip

✓ Stay focused on the enquiry.

✓ Identify **one specific detail** from the content of the source.

✓ Give a follow-up question that is linked to the detail you have chosen **and** to the enquiry in the question.

✓ Choose a type of source to help answer your follow-up question that is **specific**.

✓ Explain **precisely** how the type of source will help answer the follow-up question.

✓ Keep all parts of your answer **concise**.

✓ **Use the table** on the exam paper.

Had a look ☐ **Nearly there** ☐ **Nailed it!** ☐

Answering Question 2b

You need to understand how you can write a successful answer to Question 2b.

Reading the question

> **2b Study Source A on page 13.**
>
> How could you follow up Source A to find out more about the conditions in Whitechapel that encouraged crime?
>
> In your answer, you must give the question you would ask and the type of source you could use.
>
> Complete the table below.
>
> **(4 marks)**

Always read the question carefully before you start writing your answer.

Always check which source the question is about.

Short, 4-mark questions do not need a plan.

Steps to success

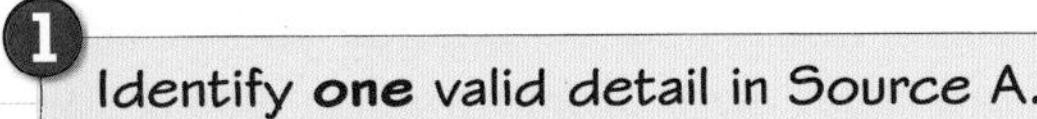

1 Identify **one** valid detail in Source A.

> Detail in Source A that I would follow up:
>
> The source says that the police would rarely patrol Wentworth Street.

Choose a specific and relevant detail from the source itself.

If the source is a text, you could quote a phrase from it.

2 Write down a follow-up question that would help you to understand the enquiry better.

> Question I would ask:
>
> Were there many parts of Whitechapel which the police would not patrol?

Make sure your question relates to the detail you have identified.

Make sure your question is also linked to the enquiry.

3 Identify a type of source that you could use to find an answer to your follow-up question.

> What type of source I could use:
>
> H Division records of police patrols by beat constables.

Give one type of source.

Choose a specific type of source. Here, just writing 'police records' would be too general.

4 Explain how your source could help you to answer your follow-up question.

> How this might help answer my question:
>
> I could plot on a map which streets were regularly patrolled, and which streets were not mentioned in the notes as much.

Make sure your explanation is related to the enquiry and the type of source you have chosen.

Make sure that you keep your explanation precise.

Had a look ☐ **Nearly there** ☐ **Nailed it!** ☐

Answering Question 2b

Getting it right

Question 2b should be a good chance to get some straightforward marks. Stay focused on the question and don't write more than you need to. Look at these examples.

Detail in Source A that I would follow up:

The source mentions that many of the people are 'bloated by drink'. **(1)**

✓ The detail given is valid – it is specific, from the source itself and it is linked to the enquiry in the question (about the conditions in Whitechapel that encouraged crime).

Question I would ask:

Were people who were arrested often drunk? **(1)**

✓ The follow-up question is connected to the detail given and to the enquiry in the question.

What type of source I could use:

Photographs

✗ This type of source is too vague. It is also not related to the follow-up question given above.

How this might help answer my question:

I could see what people looked like at the time.

✗ This is too vague and doesn't give enough explanation. It is also not related to the follow-up question given above.

Detail in Source A that I would follow up:

The source says men are 'smoking evil-smelling pipes'. **(1)**

✓ This detail is valid.

Question I would ask:

Did lots of people smoke in the 1800s?

✗ This is not a valid question because, although it's connected to the detail, it isn't related to the enquiry – about the conditions in Whitechapel that encouraged crime.

What type of source I could use:

Photographs of people in Whitechapel in the 1880s taken from newspapers.

✗ This gives a specific source, but it's linked to the follow-up question, which isn't related to the enquiry, so this wouldn't gain a mark.

How this might help answer my question:

I could look at how many people in the photographs have signs of smoking.

✗ This explanation is precise, but it's linked to the follow-up query, which isn't related to the enquiry, so it wouldn't get a mark.

Detail in Source A that I would follow up:

The source says that side streets were 'oppressively dark'. **(1)**

✓ This is a valid detail from the source which is related to the enquiry.

Question I would ask:

Did crime mainly happen in streets with no lights? **(1)**

✓ This is a valid follow-up question which is related to the detail given above **and** the enquiry.

What type of source I could use:

Crime scene photographs from police records. **(1)**

✓ This gives a specific source and is related to the enquiry.

How this might help answer my question:

I could see how many of the crime scenes had street lights, and how many were unlit. **(1)**

✓ This gives a precise explanation of how the source would help answer the follow-up question, and is related to the enquiry.

Had a look ☐ **Nearly there** ☐ **Nailed it!** ☐

Understanding Question 3

Question 3 will always be structured in the same way. Make sure you know how this question works and what it is asking you to do.

How does Question 3 work?

This tells you that you need to write about just **one** difference. This question will always ask **either** about a difference **or** a similarity.

Identify the command word – this question will always ask you to 'explain'.

> 3 Explain **one** way in which policing in the years c1700–c1900 was different from policing in the years c1900–present.
>
> **(4 marks)**

This is the topic for the question.

Check how many marks the question is worth – this will help you to manage your time.

These are the two time periods that you need to compare – the question will always give you two separate periods.

You will always need to make a comparison between two time periods – either how something was similar in the two periods, or how it was different.

What does Question 3 assess?

- Question 3 tests Assessment Objectives 1 and 2.
- You need to show your knowledge of the topic.
- You also need to show you can explain and analyse similarity or difference between two periods of time.

How long should I spend?

Spend about 5 minutes on Question 3.

Try not to spend longer than this as the next questions will need plenty of time.

Take a look at page 17 for more about the assessment objectives.

What does 'explain' mean?

For Question 3, you need to make a comparison – you need to **explain** one way in which something was similar or different over time. To do this, you need to:

- **identify a difference or a similarity** (whichever the question asks for)
- **give specific examples from each time period** to support the difference or similarity you have identified.

Remember!

- You only need to explain **one** similarity/difference.
- You need to explain **how** it was different – not why.
- You need to make sure you understand time periods and the different ways they can be written – to make sure you give examples from the right period.

You can find out more about dates on page 15.

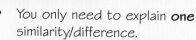

Had a look ☐ **Nearly there** ☐ **Nailed it!** ☐

Understanding Question 3

Identifying a difference/similarity

- Make sure you are clear about the topic in the question.
- Identify a difference/similarity that is **linked to the topic** in the question.
- State the difference/similarity you identify **clearly** in your answer – it is best to do this before you go on to give evidence from each time period.

If you are asked about a similarity, you need to identify something that did not change between the time periods. If you are asked about a difference, you need to identify something that did change.

Supporting your comparison

- Give **examples from each time period** to explain the difference/similarity you have identified – this is where you show your knowledge of the topic.
- Make sure the examples are **relevant** to the difference/similarity you have identified.
- Make sure your examples from each time period **link up** with each other – otherwise you are not showing a difference/similarity.

Keep your supporting information **balanced** and **specific**:

✓ Do give examples from **each** time period.

✗ Don't just say it was different/the same in the other time period.

How is Question 3 marked?

Strong answers to Question 3:

✓ analyse features of the period to explain a difference or similarity

✓ give specific information about the topic to support the comparison

✓ show good knowledge and understanding of both time periods.

Top tip

Remember to use **key terms** in your answer.

Using language to write clear answers

To make your answer clear, you could introduce the similarity or difference like this:

One way in which [the topic] was different/similar is…

You could introduce your examples like this:

In [the first period]…

In comparison, during [the second period]…

Turn to page 12 for more about writing clear answers. You can find examples of key terms on page 15.

Top tips for success

Top tip

✓ State one difference/similarity **clearly** at the beginning of your answer.

✓ Make sure your difference/similarity is **linked to the topic** in the question.

✓ Give **examples from each time period** to support your difference/similarity and keep your answer balanced.

✓ Make sure your examples are **relevant** and **specific**, and that they link up with each other.

✓ Use **key terms** to show your knowledge and understanding.

✓ Keep your answers **concise** – don't write more than you need to.

✓ Be **specific** – avoid very general, vague comparisons (like 'modern police are better').

✓ Be **accurate** – use correct facts to support your comparison.

Had a look ☐ **Nearly there** ☐ **Nailed it!** 

Answering Question 3

You need to understand how you can write a successful answer to Question 3.

Reading the question

> 3 Explain **one** way in which policing in the years c1700–c1900 was different from policing in the years c1900–present.
>
> **(4 marks)**

Always read the question carefully before you start writing your answer. Make sure you are clear about what the topic of the question is.

Short, 4-mark questions do not need a plan.

Identify which two time periods you are being asked to compare.

Check carefully whether you need to write about a similarity or a difference.

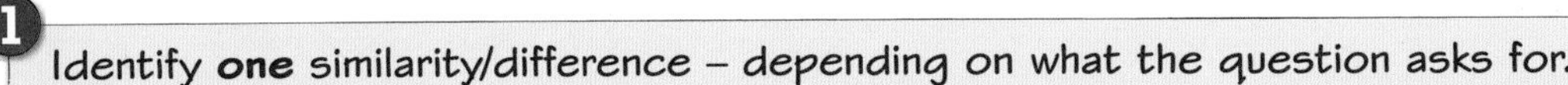

Steps to success

1 Identify **one** similarity/difference – depending on what the question asks for.

> One way in which policing was different was that police in the years c1900–present have made greater use of technology to investigate crimes.

Use clear language to focus your answer from the start.

Start by clearly stating the similarity or difference between the two periods.

2 Focus on the earlier time period. Give an example of what happened in this period.

> In the years c1700–c1900, the police did not use much technology, and what they used was basic technology, such as printing pamphlets or posters. Instead, they relied on simpler techniques, like speaking to people in the streets.

Make sure your example is relevant to the similarity or difference you have identified.

Keep your example specific and concise.

3 Focus on the later time period. Give an example of how this was similar/different to the earlier period.

> In comparison, police in the modern period use more advanced technology like CCTV footage, DNA testing and internet databases to compare case files. This makes them more effective at solving serious crimes.

Use clear language to show you are comparing the two periods. You could also use phrases such as 'However' or 'This changed when...'

Use key terms to show your knowledge of the topic.

Make sure your example is relevant to your difference or similarity.

Had a look ☐ **Nearly there** ☐ **Nailed it!** ☐

Answering Question 3

Getting it right

Question 3 should be a good chance to get some straightforward marks. Stay focused on the question and don't write more than you need to. Look at these examples.

> One way in which policing was different is that the police have become better organised in the years c1900–present. The police now have specialised departments like a Police Central e-crime Unit or a Special Branch for dealing with terrorism. A similarity is that, through the two time periods, the majority of the police were not armed with weapons, and were trained to use force as a last resort.

✓ A difference is clearly identified at the start of the answer.

✗ The answer gives an example from the later period, which is good. But there is no example from the earlier period, so the answer doesn't explain the difference.

✗ The answer discusses a similarity. The facts are correct, but the question only asks about a difference so this won't receive any marks.

> In the years c1700–c1900, the police were not very effective at their jobs and lots of criminals got away, but by the later 1900s, police forces were better at solving crimes.

✗ No clear statement of difference is given at the start of the answer.

✗ This comparison isn't supported with evidence. It needs relevant examples from each time period.

✗ This comparison is too general. Saying that something was 'better' is not specific enough.

> One way in which policing was different in these periods is that the police in the 1800s were not armed, but in the modern period armed police have become more important. In the 1800s, police uniforms were deliberately designed not to look like soldiers and this included not having guns or swords. In comparison, in the 1900s, violent crime and terrorism became more common, so modern police forces have more officers who carry guns and look like soldiers.

✓ The opening sentence clearly states a valid difference between the two time periods.

✓ This is a specific example from the earlier period which is also relevant to the difference identified in the opening statement.

✓ This specific example from the modern period creates a clear comparison and shows that equal weight is being given to both time periods.

Understanding Question 4

Question 4 will always be structured in the same way. Make sure you know how this question works and what it is asking you to do.

How does Question 4 work?

Identify the command phrase – this question will always ask you to 'explain why'.

This is the change that you need to explain.

The question will always have dates, so make sure that you write about the correct time period.

Check how many marks the question is worth – this will help you to manage your time.

> **4** Explain why there were changes in punishments in the years c1000–c1200.
>
> **(12 marks)**
>
> You may use the following in your answer:
>
> - Forest Laws
> - end of Wergild
>
> You **must** also use information of your own.

Look at the two suggestions – they might be helpful in deciding what to write about.

You **must** include at least one reason from your own knowledge.

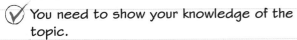

This question is similar to Question 1b on Paper 2 (your British depth study) and Question 2 on Paper 3 (your modern depth study).

What does Question 4 assess?

- Question 4 tests Assessment Objectives 1 and 2.
- You need to show your knowledge of the topic.
- You also need to explain and analyse what caused change to happen.

Take a look at page 17 for more about the assessment objectives.

How long should I spend?

Spend about 18 minutes on Question 4.

This question is worth 12 marks so leave yourself enough time to do a good job. But don't spend too long – you will need enough time for the 16-mark essay question.

What does 'explain why' mean?

Explaining why means giving reasons for something. It is different to just describing a topic. For example, if you were asked 'what was school like today?' you would describe your day. But, if you were asked 'why did you go to school today?' you would give reasons why you went to school. It is the same with this question – you need to write an analysis, giving three reasons that explain why the change in the question happened.

What will Question 4 focus on?

Question 4 could ask you about any aspect of crime and punishment in Britain that you have studied. It will cover a broad topic, such as changing punishments, over a large timescale. The question will ask you to explain the reasons why something changed or why it stayed the same.

Top tip

The key thing to remember is that you need three reasons and each one needs to be connected to the question topic.

Had a look ☐ **Nearly there** ☐ **Nailed it!** ☐

Understanding Question 4

Choosing reasons

Question 4 will always include two bullet points. **These bullet points are only suggestions – you don't have to use them.** This type of question will always have several possible reasons. So, if you don't know what one of the bullet points means, or you don't feel confident writing a paragraph about it, you can replace it with a reason of your own.

For example, the question on page 35 suggests 'Forest Laws' and 'end of Wergild'. If you were answering this question, you could write about these reasons. However, you need **three** reasons in your answer, so you would need to add at least one idea of your own – for example, William's need to end rebellions against his authority.

Remember: Even if you replace one or both bullet points with another reason, you still need to give **three reasons** overall. At least one of the reasons needs to be your own information.

How is Question 4 marked?

Strong answers to Question 4:

- ✓ give an analytical explanation which is tightly focused on the question throughout
- ✓ keep their explanation clear and well-organised throughout
- ✓ include information that is accurate, relevant and closely linked to the question
- ✓ show a wide range of knowledge and understanding of the topic.

Using language to write clear answers

To make your answer clear, you could start each paragraph like this:

One reason was…

A second reason was…

A third reason was…

Writing analytically

You need to make sure you are **explaining why**. This is called writing analytically. Use phrases like these to show how each reason led to the change in the question:

- This led to…
- As a result…
- Consequently…
- This increased/reduced…
- This showed that…

Top tip

Remember to use **key terms** in your answer.

Turn to page 12 for more about writing clear answers. You can find examples of key terms on page 15.

You don't need to write an introduction or a conclusion for Question 4.

Top tips for success

Top tip

- ✓ Give **three reasons** in your explanation.
- ✓ Include **information of your own.**
- ✓ **Plan** your answer before you write – this will help you to stay focused on the question throughout your answer.
- ✓ Structure your answer clearly using **PEEL paragraphs.**
- ✓ **Explain clearly** why each reason you include caused the change in the question.
- ✓ Support each reason with **clear and accurate information** about the topic.
- ✓ Make sure you stick to the date range given in the question – only include information from that period.

Had a look ☐ **Nearly there** ☐ **Nailed it!** ☐

Answering Question 4

You need to understand how you can write a successful answer to Question 4.

Reading the question

> **4** Explain why there were changes in punishments in the years c1000–c1200.
>
> **(12 marks)**
>
> You may use the following in your answer:
> - Forest Laws
> - end of Wergild
>
> You **must** also use information of your own.

Always read the question carefully before you start writing your answer. Make sure you are clear on the topic.

Check the number of marks. This will help you to use your time well in the exam.

How can I structure my answer?

1. Write about your first reason in one PEEL paragraph.

2. Write about your second reason in one PEEL paragraph.
3. Write about your third reason in one PEEL paragraph.

Remember **PEEL: Point – Evidence – Explain – Link**

You can find out more about paragraphing and the PEEL structure on page 12.

Plan your answer

This question is worth 12 marks, so take a minute or two to make a quick plan before you start writing.

1. Forest Laws
   - Hunting and collecting wood = new crimes against king's property
   - Harsh penalties needed, e.g. castration
2. End of Wergild
   - Wergild paid to victims but William needed money
   - New fines system = money paid to William
3. William needed to control Anglo-Saxons
   - Norman invasion = danger of A-S rebellion
   - Protect Normans = murdrum

Number the points in your plan so you have an order for your answer.

The best answers are well-organised, with three paragraphs. Structure your plan to reflect this.

Remember to include your own knowledge in the plan. This plan includes a third reason which was not mentioned in the question.

Keep your plan short and simple. You don't need to write in full sentences.

This is one style of plan. You can see another style on page 68.

Had a look ☐ **Nearly there** ☐ **Nailed it!** ☐

Answering Question 4

Steps to success

1 Write a paragraph about your first point. Remember to use PEEL to structure your paragraph clearly.

One reason that there were changes in punishments in this period was the introduction of the new Forest Laws. The creation of new 'Royal Forests' meant that hunting or collecting wood without a license became crimes against royal property. These crimes were common as people relied on hunting for food. Because these crimes were crimes against the king's property they were seen as a challenge to William I's authority. As a result, new, harsher penalties, such as blinding and castration, were introduced to deal with these kinds of new crimes. Therefore, the new laws and new crimes led to new punishments.

Make a clear **point** at the start to show what the paragraph is about. This example uses one of the reasons given in the question.

Include some **evidence**. This example only uses a couple of specific facts but it is enough to show understanding of the topic.

Explain how the reason caused the change (here, the change in punishments).

Link back to the question.

2 Write a paragraph about your second point. Keep focused on the question and use PEEL to structure your writing.

A second reason was that William I ended Wergild because it did not meet his needs. William needed to fund his monarchy and establish his authority, so he needed money. Wergild was a system of fines where money was paid straight to the victim or their family. However, this meant that Wergild did not benefit the authorities. As a result, William replaced Wergild with a system of fines which were paid to his officials instead. Before 1066, Wergild had been an important Anglo-Saxon punishment. Consequently, William's action was a major change to punishments.

Make a second **point**. You could use the other reason given in the question.

Give **evidence** to support your point.

Explain – here, the phrase 'this meant that' is used to write analytically.

Link back to the question.

3 Write a paragraph about your third point. Remember to refer back to your plan and stay focused on explaining why.

A third reason was that William needed to stop the Anglo-Saxons from rebelling against Norman control...

As a result, the murdrum fine was introduced...

This led to a change in punishments because...

Always include **three** reasons. This paragraph is about a reason that was not suggested in the question – so it also uses own knowledge.

Had a look ☐ **Nearly there** ☐ **Nailed it!** ☐

Understanding Question 5/6

Question 5/6 will always be structured in the same way. Make sure you know how this question works and what it is asking you to do.

How does Question 5/6 work?

Identify the command phrase – 'how far' means you need to make a judgement. You also need to explain and justify your judgement.

Check how many marks the question is worth – this will help you to manage your time.

Look at the two factors suggested – they might be helpful in deciding what to write about.

Identify the opinion in the statement – this question will always start with an opinion about something.

5/6 'The abolition of the death penalty in 1998 was the most significant change to punishment in the years c1800–present.'

How far do you agree? Explain your answer.

(16 marks plus 4 marks for SPaG and use of specialist terminology)

You may use the following in your answer:

- the Derek Bentley case, 1953
- the use of ASBOs and electronic tagging

You **must** also use information of your own.

Up to four of the marks of the total for this question will be awarded for good use of spelling, punctuation and grammar, and for use of specialist terminology. You can find out about key terms and SPaG on pages 15 and 16.

You **must** use your own information – this includes writing about at least one factor that is not given in the question.

In the exam, you will have a choice of two questions – you must answer **either** Question 5 **or** Question 6. Both of them will be structured like this example.

Links This question is similar to Question 1c on Paper 2 (your British depth study).

What does Question 5/6 assess?

- Question 5/6 tests Assessment Objectives 1 and 2.
- You need to show your knowledge of the topic.
- You also need to show you can explain and analyse events using second-order concepts such as causation and change.

How long should I spend?

Spend about 25 minutes on Question 5/6.

This question is worth more marks than any other question on your exam paper, so make sure you leave yourself enough time to finish your answer.

Take a look at page 17 for more about the assessment objectives.

Analysing the statement

Make sure you understand the statement.

- Identify what the question is about – the example above is about the abolition of the death penalty.
- **Identify the opinion clearly** – in the example above, the opinion is that the abolition of the death penalty was the most significant change to punishment in the years c1800–present.

Choosing factors to write about

Question 5/6 will always include two bullet points. **These bullet points are only suggestions of factors you could use to support or challenge the statement – you don't have to use them.** If you don't know what one of the bullet points means, or you don't feel confident writing about it, you can choose to write about another factor.

Had a look ☐ **Nearly there** ☐ **Nailed it!** ☐

Understanding Question 5/6

'How far do you agree?'

You need to reach a judgement about the statement in the question.

- Look at evidence that agrees with the statement **and** at evidence that challenges it.
- Use your knowledge to reach a final judgement – don't just write down everything you know about the topic.
- Explain why you have made that judgement.

Your overall judgement

Your overall judgement needs to be justified – you need to include a reason for your decision. In your overall judgement, make sure you:

- **Say how far you agree** with the statement – for example, 'Overall, I agree...'
- **Give a clear reason** for your opinion by comparing the factors in a short summary at the end of your answer.

How is Question 5/6 marked?

Strong answers to Question 5/6:

- ✓ give an analytical explanation which is tightly focused on the question throughout
- ✓ keep their explanation clear and well-organised throughout
- ✓ include information that is accurate, relevant and closely linked to the question
- ✓ show a wide range of knowledge and understanding of the topic
- ✓ reach an overall judgement which is fully justified
- ✓ use correct spelling, punctuation and grammar and specialist terms.

Writing analytically

Use phrases that show you are explaining the opinion in the statement and making a judgement about that viewpoint. This is called 'writing analytically'. For example:

- I agree/do not agree...
- Although I agree to a certain extent... it is also true that...
- The viewpoint in the statement is valid because...
- This can be supported by...

Top tip

Remember to use **key terms** in your answer.

Turn to page 12 for more about writing clear answers. You can find examples of key terms on page 15.

You **will** need to write an introduction and conclusion for Question 5/6.

Top tips for success

Top tip

- ✓ **Plan** your answer before you write to help you to stay focused on the question.
- ✓ Start with a **short introduction** – say what you will cover in your answer.
- ✓ Include **arguments for the statement** in the question and **counter-arguments**.
- ✓ Use **clear and accurate evidence** to support your arguments.
- ✓ **Explain clearly why** your evidence supports or challenges the statement – don't just describe the factor you are writing about.
- ✓ **Link factors together and compare them** to say which is more important.
- ✓ Use **information of your own** – at least one factor not given in the question.
- ✓ Structure your answer clearly using **PEEL paragraphs**.
- ✓ If the question includes a date range (for example, 'c1800–present'), only include information from that period.
- ✓ Use correct **spelling, punctuation, grammar** and **specialist terminology**.
- ✓ End with an **overall judgement** about how far you agree with the statement.

Had a look ☐ **Nearly there** ☐ **Nailed it!** ☐

Answering Question 5/6

You need to understand how you can write a successful answer to Question 5/6.

Reading the question

5/6 'The abolition of the death penalty in 1998 was the most significant change to punishment in the years c1800–present.'

How far do you agree? Explain your answer.

(16 marks plus 4 marks for SPaG and use of specialist terminology)

You may use the following in your answer:

- the Derek Bentley case, 1953
- the use of ASBOs and electronic tagging

You **must** also use information of your own.

Always read the question carefully before you start writing your answer.

Make sure you identify the opinion in the statement.

Remember that up to four marks are available for the quality of your writing.

Use **PEEL** paragraphs.

See page 12 for more about paragraphing and PEEL.

How can I structure my answer?

1 Write a short introduction. Say what the question is about and what you will write about.

2 Begin your argument. You could start by writing about evidence that supports the statement.

3 Continue your argument. If you started with evidence that supports the statement, move on to write about other factors that challenge the statement.

4 Write a conclusion. Give an overall judgement and explain why you reached that decision.

Plan your answer

This question is worth 16 marks, so take the time to make a good plan before you start writing.

Support	Challenge
1. Showed change in public attitude • Bentley case 1953 • Made prison more important	2. Prisons = more rehab • Separate system • Education programmes 3. Alternative punishments • ASBOs & tagging • Community projects
Judgement: Mostly disagree – abolition = big change but rehabilitation affected more criminals.	

The best answers are structured logically. List factors that support and challenge the statement.

Include your own knowledge. This factor was not mentioned in the question.

Add specific evidence and facts.

Make a judgement and include it in the plan to help you stay focused.

Had a look ☐ **Nearly there** ☐ **Nailed it!** ☐

Answering Question 5/6

Steps to success

1 Write a short introduction. Say what the question is about and what you will write about.

The abolition of the death penalty was a significant change to punishment in the years c1800–present. There were also other important changes, including changes to the prison system and the development of alternatives. I think the introduction of punishments aimed at rehabilitation was most significant.

Identify what the question is about. Use words from the statement.

Indicate the viewpoints that you will cover.

Make a judgement here to focus your answer.

2 Begin your argument. You could start by writing about evidence that supports the statement.

The death penalty was last used in 1964 and fully abolished in 1998. This was a significant change because it showed a change of public attitude. For example, in 1953, Derek Bentley was hanged for his part in the death of a police officer, even though he had not fired the gun himself. In the 1800s, people would not have been as concerned over the execution of a criminal, but in Bentley's case there was a huge public outcry and the media was sympathetic. Therefore, the last use of the death penalty just a few years later is important in showing a change in attitude to punishments. …

Use clear language to identify the **point**.

Use your knowledge to give **evidence**.

Explain how your evidence supports your point.

Link back to the question.

3 Continue your argument. If you started with evidence that supports the statement, move on to write about other factors – as in this example.

However, while I agree that the abolition of the death penalty was important, there were other changes to punishment that were more important. For example, changes to the prison system made rehabilitation more important than deterrence…

Always include a **counter-argument**. Signpost it clearly.

Use phrases that show you are making a judgement.

Include information that is not given in the question, like this factor.

4 Write a conclusion. Give an overall judgement about how far you agree with the statement.

Overall, I mostly disagree with the statement. Although the abolition of the death penalty showed a significant change in attitude, most criminals would not have been executed. In contrast, ideas about rehabilitation and alternative punishments affected many more. Consequently, these changes were more significant.

Give your overall judgement on the statement. You could also start with 'In conclusion…'

Explain your overall judgement by comparing the factors you have considered.

Had a look ☐ **Nearly there** ☐ **Nailed it!** ☐

This is how long you have to answer all the questions for your Paper 1 thematic study and historic environment in the exam.

In the exam, the sources you need are in a separate booklet.
Here, you can find the sources on page 61.

Get used to writing with a black pen.

In the exam, there will be spaces for you to do this.

Check carefully which questions you must answer, and where you have a choice.

Focus on answering the question fully, rather than trying to fill all the writing lines.

Use the marks to help you work out how long to spend on each question.

Pearson Edexcel GCSE (9–1)

History

Paper 1: Thematic study and historic environment

Option 10: Crime and punishment in Britain, c1000–present *and* Whitechapel, c1870–c1900: crime, policing and the inner city

Time: 1 hour 15 minutes

You must have: Sources Booklet.

Instructions

- Use **black** ink or ball-point pen.
- **Fill in** your name, centre number and candidate number.
- There are two sections in this question paper. Answer Questions 1 and 2 from Section A. From Section B, answer Questions 3 and 4 and then **EITHER** Question 5 **OR** Question 6.
- Answer the questions in the spaces provided – there may be more space than you need.

Information

- The total mark for this paper is 52.
- The marks for **each** question are shown in brackets.
- The marks available for spelling, punctuation, grammar and use of specialist terminology are clearly indicated.

In Paper 1, it is Question 5/6 that has additional marks available for SPaG and use of specialist terminology.

Top tip

Make sure you:

- read each question carefully before you start writing your answer
- try to answer every question
- save about five minutes to check your answers at the end.

SECTION A: Whitechapel, c1870–c1900: crime, policing and the inner city
Answer Questions 1 and 2.

Describe **two** features of the immigrant population of Whitechapel.

(4 marks)

Feature 1

....

....

....

....

....

....

Feature 2

....

....

....

....

....

....

Time

Spend **about 5 minutes** on this question.

Unlocking the question

A **feature** means any relevant, accurate detail about the topic.

Unlocking the question

Describe means say what the features are. You don't need to give reasons for the features or say how important they were.

Revision Guide

Revise this topic on page 27.

Watch out!

Make sure you describe **two different features**.

LEARN IT!

Use phrases like 'One feature was…' to make your answer clear.

Hint

Add **relevant supporting information** to each feature.

Hint

Use **key terms** to show your topic knowledge.

Top tip

Keep your answer **specific**, **accurate** and **concise**.

Time

Spend **about 14 minutes** on this question.

Top tip

Note down a **quick** plan. Include points you will make for each source.

Revision Guide

Revise this topic on pages 26–29.

Unlocking the question

You need to make a judgement about **how useful** each source is **for the enquiry** in the question.

Unlocking the question

You must refer to **both sources** and use your **own knowledge** in your answer.

Unlocking the question

Usefulness is about what the source tells you about the enquiry and how accurate it is.

Unlocking the question

You need to consider both the **content** and **provenance** of each source and **explain** why this makes the source more or less useful.

Top tip

Structure your answer clearly. Write about one source, then the other.

2a Study Sources A and B on page 61.

How useful are Sources A and B for an enquiry into the difficulties faced by the police in the Whitechapel area?

Explain your answer, using Sources A and B and your knowledge of the historical context.

(8 marks)

LEARN IT!

Remember: provenance is **nature**, **origin** and **purpose**.

Watch out!

Make sure you stay focused on the enquiry in the question.

Watch out!

You don't need to compare the sources or decide which one is more useful.

Hint

Compare the source with your **own knowledge**. Does the source support what you know?

Hint

A source which is **accurate and balanced** is usually more useful than one that is exaggerated and one-sided.

Watch out!

Don't say a source is useless – no source in the exam will ever be useless for the enquiry.

LEARN IT!

Use phrases such as 'not very useful' and 'very useful' to show your opinion of each source.

Hint

Think about whether the information in the source is **accurate**. Is it balanced?

Time

Spend **about 5 minutes** on this question.

Unlocking the question

This question will only ask about **one** source. Look at the right one.

Unlocking the question

The enquiry in the question will always be the same as the enquiry in Question 2a.

Hint

Use the table structure to help keep your answer concise.

Hint

Choose **one** detail from the source that is **specific** and **relevant to the enquiry** in the question.

Top tip

If it's a written source, **quote** a detail from it.

Watch out!

Your follow-up question **must** be linked to the detail you have identified **and** the enquiry.

Hint

The type of source must help to answer your follow-up question and must be **specific**.

Hint

Your explanation must be **precise**.

2b Study Source A on page 61.

How could you follow up Source A to find out more about the difficultie faced by the police in the Whitechapel area?

In your answer, you must give the question you would ask and the type source you could use.

Complete the table below.

(4 marl

Detail in Source A that I would follow up:

Question I would ask:

What type of source I could use:

How this might help answer my question:

SECTION B: Crime and punishment in Britain, c1000–present

Answer Questions 3 and 4. Then answer EITHER Question 5 OR Question 6.

Explain **one** way in which the role of local communities in law enforcement was similar in the medieval period (c1000–c1500) and the early modern period (c1500–c1700).

(4 marks)

....

....

....

....

....

....

....

....

....

....

....

....

....

Time

Spend **about 5 minutes** on this question.

Unlocking the question

You need to provide details of **one** way in which something was **similar or different**.

Watch out!

Don't write about a difference if the question asks about a similarity – and vice versa.

Revision Guide

Revise this topic on pages 4 and 9.

Top tip

State the difference/similarity clearly at the **beginning** of your answer.

Watch out!

Make sure your difference/similarity is linked to the topic in the question.

Watch out!

Focus on **how** it was different/similar, not why.

Hint

Make your supporting information balanced – give examples for **each** time period.

Watch out!

Keep your examples **specific** and **relevant** to your difference/similarity.

Spend **about 18 minutes** on this question.

Top tip

Always start 12-mark questions with a quick plan. Use the Notes pages at the back of this book if you need extra space – but keep your plan **short**.

Unlocking the question

The command phrase in this question will always be 'explain why' so you will always have to **give reasons** for something happening or not happening.

Unlocking the question

The bullet points give you suggestions about what to write about, but you don't have to use them if you don't want to.

Unlocking the question

You **must** include at least one reason from your own knowledge.

Revision Guide

Revise this topic on pages 6, 7 and 9.

Hint

Start each paragraph with phrases like, 'One reason is...', 'A second reason is...' and so on, to make your answer clear.

4 Explain why there were changes in the role of the Church in crime and punishment in the period c1000–c1700.

(12 marks)

You may use the following in your answer:

- Church courts
- heresy

You **must** also use information of your own.

....

....

....

....

....

....

....

....

....

....

....

....

....

....

....

....

....

....

....

....

....

....

....

....

....

....

....

Hint

You don't need to write an introduction or a conclusion for this answer.

Watch out!

You **must** stick to the date range given in the question.

Hint

Support each reason with **clear and accurate information** about the topic.

Watch out!

You **don't** have to decide which reason was more important.

Aim higher

Make sure your explanation is analytical and keep it tightly focused on the question throughout the answer.

Hint

Use **key terms**, like names, dates or specific examples to support each reason you give.

LEARN IT!

Structure your answer clearly. Use a separate **PEEL (Point – Evidence – Explain – Link)** paragraph to write about each reason.

Hint

Use phrases like 'as a result…', 'consequently…' or 'this caused…' to focus your answer and show you are writing **analytically**.

Top tip

You need to include **three** reasons in your answer and each one needs to be connected to the question topic.

Watch out!

For each reason you have given, make sure you explain clearly **why** it caused the change or event in the question. Don't just describe the topic.

Aim higher

Remember: changes can happen because of events, ideas or attitudes.

Top tip

When you have finished writing, read back through your answer. Check that you have included examples and details to back up your points, and that you have explained why each point led to the change or event in the question.

Answer EITHER Question 5 OR Question 6.
Spelling, punctuation, grammar and use of specialist terminology will be assessed in this question.

THER

'The move towards prevention was the most important change to law enforcement in the years c1700–present.'

How far do you agree? Explain your answer.

(16 marks plus 4 marks for SPaG and use of specialist terminology)

You may use the following in your answer:

- Bow Street Runners
- Neighbourhood Watch

You **must** also use information of your own.

R

'Crimes against property were the greatest challenge to the government in the period c1000–c1700.'

How far do you agree? Explain your answer.

(16 marks plus 4 marks for SPaG and use of specialist terminology)

You may use the following in your answer:

- poaching
- the Gunpowder Plot (1605)

You **must** also use information of your own.

Time

Remember that this question is worth more marks than the other questions on your thematic study. Make sure you leave enough time to answer it fully.

Watch out!

In the exam, you only need to answer **one** of these questions. Don't try to answer both!

Unlocking the question

Look carefully at each option, including the suggestions in the bullet points, and consider how much you know about each topic. Choose the option you feel you can write most about.

Top tip

It is worth spending a short time carefully picking the question before you start writing. This way you are more likely to pick the question you can answer best, which will save you time overall.

Revision Guide

For Question 5, revise changes in law enforcement on pages 15 and 21.

Revision Guide

For Question 6, revise crimes that challenged the government on pages 1, 8, 11 and 13–14.

Watch out!

In the exam, you should only answer **either** Question 5 **or** Question 6. In this practice paper there is space for you to have a go at both options.

Hint

Use this space to answer Question 5.

Time

Spend **about 25 minutes** on this question.

Top tip

Always start 16-mark questions with a good plan.

Unlocking the question

You need to reach a **clear judgement** in your answer.

Unlocking the question

Identify the opinion in the question before you start writing. You need to know what you need to reach a judgement about.

Hint

In a short introduction, summarise the question and what you will mention in the answer.

Aim higher

State your judgement in the introduction – this will help you to keep your answer focused.

Indicate which question you are answering by marking a cross in the box ☒. If you change your mind, put a line through the box ☒ and then indicate your new question with a cross ☒.

Chosen question number:

Question 5 ☒

Question 6 ☒

Top tip

Structure your answer clearly. Either start by writing about information that supports the statement, or information that challenges it.

Unlocking the question

You don't have to use the two bullet points, but they might help you decide what to write about.

Unlocking the question

You **must** include **at least one factor** that is not mentioned in the question.

Unlocking the question

It doesn't matter whether you agree or disagree with the statement – your answer still needs to consider evidence that supports the statement **and** evidence that challenges it.

Unlocking the question

This question assesses your **spelling, punctuation, grammar** and **use of specialist terms**.

Watch out!

Don't just give your opinion. Make sure you **explain** why you have reached your judgement.

Top tip

Use **PEEL (Point – Evidence – Explain – Link)** paragraphs to organise each main point.

Hint

Link each point of evidence to the question. Use phrases like 'this shows that…'

Watch out!

Avoid making general statements. Use **specific and accurate** examples.

Hint

Each point you make should clearly support or challenge the statement in the question.

Watch out!

Make sure you stick to the **time period** the question is asking about.

LEARN IT!

Use language to show you are **explaining** the opinion in the statement and making a **judgement** about it – such as, 'The viewpoint is valid because…'

Watch out!

Don't just describe the topic. Be clear about how your examples support or challenge the statement.

Hint

Use **key terms** to show your topic knowledge.

LEARN IT!

Practise any spellings you know you find tricky. This will help you to write an answer that is strong in SPaG.

Aim higher

Link the factors together. One place to do this is in the conclusion.

Aim higher

Compare the factors to show which are more important, or which had an impact on other factors.

Hint

Your conclusion must reach a **clear judgement**.

Hint

You could start your conclusion with 'Overall, I...' or 'In conclusion...'

Watch out!

You need to state how far you agree with the statement **and** explain why you have reached this judgement.

Top tip

To explain your judgement clearly, think about **why** you have reached that opinion. For example, did one factor have more effect than other factors?

Watch out!

In the exam, you should only answer **either** Question 5 **or** Question 6. In this practice paper there is space for you to have a go at both options.

Hint

Use this space to answer Question 6.

Time

Spend **about 25 minutes** on this question.

Top tip

Always start 16-mark questions with a good plan. Use the Notes pages at the back of this book if you need extra space.

Unlocking the question

Identify the opinion in the question before you start writing. You need to know what you need to reach a judgement about.

Hint

Start with an **introduction** – give a short summary of what you are going to write about.

Aim higher

Decide on your judgement before you start writing. This will help you to write a more focused **analytical** explanation.

Indicate which question you are answering by marking a cross in the box ☒. If you change your mind, put a line through the box ☒ and then indicate your new question with a cross ☒.

Chosen question number:

Question 5 ☒

Question 6 ☒

Unlocking the question

Look at the two bullet points. They will help you decide what to include in your answer.

Unlocking the question

You **must** include **at least one factor** that is not mentioned in the question.

Unlocking the question

You need to consider evidence that supports the statement **and** evidence that challenges it.

Unlocking the question

Pay attention to the **quality of your writing** for this answer. This question has additional marks available for SPaG and use of specialist terms.

Top tip

Structure your answer clearly. Either start by writing about information that supports the statement or information that challenges it.

Aim higher

You don't need to wait until the conclusion to show your judgement. As you write about a factor, use phrases like 'this was more/less important because…' to explain your viewpoint.

Hint

Once you have written about your evidence that supports or challenges the statement, write your **counter-argument**.

Top tip

Use **PEEL (Point – Evidence – Explain – Link)** paragraphs to organise each main point.

Watch out!

Stay focused. **Link** each point of evidence back to the question to avoid going off the topic.

Aim higher

Include **specific, accurate details** to back up each main point – for example, details of people, events and dates.

Top tip

As you write, look back at the question occasionally. This will help you to stay focused on the question.

Watch out!

Make sure you stick to the **time period** the question is asking about.

Top tip

Start each paragraph with **clear language** that focuses what you are writing. For example, you could write 'Another example that supports/challenges the statement is…'

Watch out!

You need to **explain why** your evidence supports or challenges the statement. Don't just describe what you know.

LEARN IT!

Show you are **explaining** the opinion in the statement and making a **judgement** about it by using phrases like 'The viewpoint is valid because...', 'However, it is also true that...', 'This can be supported by...'

LEARN IT!

Practise tricky spellings and get used to starting and ending your sentences clearly. This will help you to write an answer that is strong in SPaG.

Hint

Always finish Question 5/6 with a conclusion that gives an **overall judgement** that is fully justified.

Hint

You could start your conclusion with 'Overall, I...' or 'In conclusion...'

Top tip

Double-check your conclusion. What reason have you given for your judgement? Make sure it is **clear and specific**.

Sources for use with Section A.

Source A: Part of a letter from James Munro, Head of the CID, to the Home Secretary, 11 September 1889. Munro is asking the Home Secretary for more support following a violent murder in Whitechapel.

> Notwithstanding every precaution, the murderer has been able to slip through our patrols, and dispose of the body of his victim without being observed by police. All that I can do is to strengthen the force of police in the locality, and make it more difficult than before for these lamentable occurrences[1] to take place. For this purpose I shall require 100 more men, both uniform and plain clothes. I cannot possibly arrange for their transfer from other Divisions which have already furnished men for the East End. The number of men applied for is absolutely necessary.

[1]**lamentable occurrences:** sad events

Source B: A cartoon published 22 September 1888, in the magazine *Punch*. *Punch* was read by middle-class families and was famous for critical cartoons. It is showing a policeman looking for criminals. In the caption, 'blind-man's buff' is a game played by children.

BLIND-MAN'S BUFF.

(*As played by the Police.*)

"TURN ROUND THREE TIMES, AND CATCH WHOM YOU MAY!"

SECTION A: Whitechapel, c1870–c1900: crime, policing and the inner city
Answer Questions 1 and 2.

Describe **two** features of the immigrant population of Whitechapel.

(4 marks)

Feature 1

One feature was that Irish immigrants made up one large group living in Whitechapel. Many of the Irish immigrants were working as navvies or dock workers.

Feature 2

A second feature was that many of the immigrants in Whitechapel were Jews from Eastern Europe. Many of them had moved to avoid religious persecution in Russia after the assassination of the Russian tsar.

Answer uses writing spaces provided.

This is a valid feature.

Supporting information gives more detail about the feature.

Second feature is valid, and different from the first.

Supporting information gives more detail about the second feature.

Answer is kept concise and examples are specific and accurate.

ternative answers

ıswers to Question 1 could also include:

- Many immigrants could only find work in sweatshops. **(1)** In the sweatshops, they made textiles for low wages, which angered local workers who charged more. **(1)**
- There was a mix of nationalities from different places. **(1)** For example, there were large numbers of Irish and Eastern European immigrants. **(1)**
- Some immigrants brought ideas which seemed dangerous to many. **(1)** For example, people associated Irish immigrants with Fenians and Eastern Europeans were associated with anarchism or socialism. **(1)**

Hint

Turn to page 61 to remind yourself about Sources A and B.

Hint

Read the notes below, then look at the sample answer on page 64.

2a Study Sources A and B on page 61.

How useful are Sources A and B for an enquiry into the difficulties faced by the police in the Whitechapel area?

Explain your answer, using Sources A and B and your knowledge of the historical context.

(8 marks)

Writing a good answer

Good answers will:

- judge the usefulness of each source for the enquiry given in the question
- explain clearly how the provenance of each source makes it more or less useful
- support their judgements with comments on the content and the provenance of each source
- use own knowledge to interpret the sources and support their judgements.

Relevant points about Source A may include:

- The source describes a shortage of police officers and how easy it is to avoid being caught by the police.
- The source is useful because it gives details of a real problem caused by not having enough police officers.
- The source is a letter written to persuade the Home Secretary to send more men, so the truth may be exaggerated.
- It was written at a time when the police in Whitechapel were under great pressure because of the recent Ripper murders.

Relevant points about Source B may include:

- The cartoon mocks the police, by showing how criminals could easily avoid being caught.
- The cartoon shows that the locals in Whitechapel did not support the police.
- The cartoon uses humour to entertain the readers of *Punch* and it does this by suggesting that the police are incompetent.
- The purpose of the cartoon is also to sell copies of *Punch*, so criticising the police is likely to be more important than accuracy.

Q2a: sample answer

Plan:

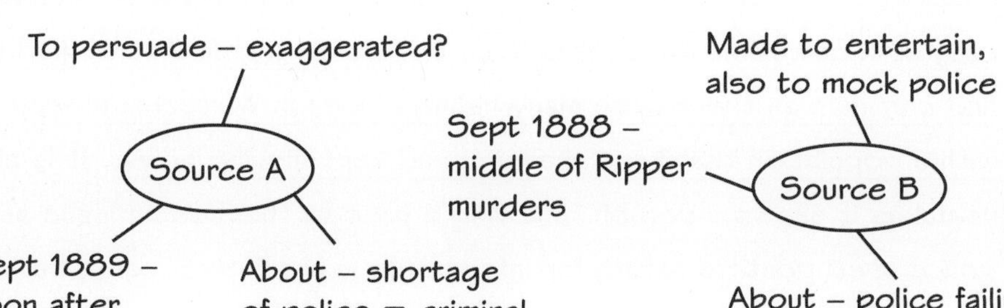

Source A is quite useful for an enquiry into the difficulties the police faced in Whitechapel. It says that a murderer was able to 'slip through our patrols, and dispose of the body', which shows that the police struggled to catch criminals in Whitechapel. The source also states that there were not enough police in Whitechapel, as the letter is asking for '100 more men', even though they had already had reinforcements. I know that H Division received officers from A Division and the City of London police. This source shows that there were still not enough officers to prevent a murderer from being able to 'dispose of the body'. This was because of the winding rookeries and alleys in Whitechapel. Source A is probably exaggerated because it is written by the head of the CID, and he is trying to persuade the Home Secretary using phrases like 'lamentable occurrences' to send more men, which would have been expensive. However, the fact that Munro is trying so hard to persuade the Home Secretary actually makes the source more useful for investigating difficulties in policing as it shows that the problems facing the police were serious enough that they needed more help. Therefore, this is a quite useful source for the enquiry.

Hint

Look at this sample answer to Question 2a. Refer back to the notes on page 63, then look to see how some of the points are used.

Quick plan helps to make answer clear and focused.

Answer looks at one source at a time, giving clear structure.

Begins with clear judgement about first source.

Analyses content of first source, staying focused on enquiry topic.

Compares source content to own knowledge.

Short quotations used to support points.

Use of key terms shows strong knowledge of topic.

Analyses provenance of first source and explains effect on usefulness.

Finishes analysis of first source with overall judgement about its usefulness.

Content and provenance of second source analysed.

Language used shows focus on giving clear judgement.

Uses own knowledge to explain how source content fits with enquiry topic.

Considers accuracy and reliability of source and how this affects usefulness.

Gives clear reason for overall judgement about second source.

Source B is partially useful because it shows a blindfolded policeman, which suggests that people thought the police were incompetent. The caption 'blind-man's buff' also suggests that avoiding the police was as easy as a children's game. It is accurate that the police struggled to find criminals as there were many hiding places in Whitechapel, combined with a population that kept changing and kept moving house. It is also useful as it shows a person removing a poster. This was an issue as the police used posters asking for information in the Ripper case, but many locals did not respond well as they disliked the police. The usefulness of Source B is limited because it was made to entertain the middle-class readers of 'Punch'. It makes the difficulties faced by the police seem very simple. I know that many middle-class people thought the police were failing in the Ripper case, and the cartoon is using that opinion to entertain because it was made in the middle of the Ripper case when the crimes were all over the newspapers. I also know that the media liked to present the police as more incompetent than they were. Overall, this source is only partially useful. It does show some difficulties the police faced but it is not reliable because it mocks them for entertainment.

A very strong answer because...

This answer comes to a clear judgement about the usefulness of each source for the given enquiry. Relevant information from both the content and provenance of each source are used to support these judgements. The student also uses their own knowledge to judge the reliability of the sources and support their judgements. The sources are given equal attention and the answer is structured clearly, with one source analysed first and then the other. Starting with a quick plan has helped the student to keep their answer tightly focused on the question throughout.

b Study Source A on page 61.

How could you follow up Source A to find out more about the difficulties faced by the police in the Whitechapel area?

In your answer, you must give the question you would ask and the type of source you could use.

Complete the table below.

(4 marks)

Detail in Source A that I would follow up:

It says that they need '100 more men'.

Question I would ask:

How many men did the CID and H Division have in Whitechapel?

What type of source I could use:

The police financial records of officers' wages.

How this might help answer my question:

I would be able to see how many officers were being paid which would tell me how many were assigned to H Division in Whitechapel.

Answer kept concise.

Detail chosen is specific, relevant to the enquiry and from the source itself, not the provenance.

Includes direct quotation from the source.

Follow-up question directly relates to detail selected from source as well as to the enquiry in the question.

Answer spaces used correctly, making answer clear.

Type of source is specific and relates to follow-up question given.

Precise explanation of how the type of source chosen would help to answer the follow-up question.

Hint

Turn to page 61 to remind yourself about Source A.

ernative nswers

other answer to Question 2b might be:

Detail in Source A that I would follow up: It says that the murderer was 'able to slip through our patrols'. **(1)**

Question I would ask: How many murderers did H Division manage to catch in the 1880s? **(1)**

What type of source I could use: The police arrest records for H Division during the 1880s. **(1)**

How this might help answer my question: I would be able to see how many times people were arrested and charged with murder. **(1)**

Hint

Read the notes below, then look at the sample answer that follows.

SECTION B: Crime and punishment in Britain, c1000–present
Answer Questions 3 and 4. Then answer EITHER Question 5 OR Question 6.

3 Explain **one** way in which the role of local communities in law enforcement was similar in the medieval period (c1000–c1500) and the early modern period (c1500–c1700).

(4 marks

Writing a good answer

Good answers will:

- analyse features of the period to explain a difference or similarity
- give specific information about the topic to support the comparison
- show good knowledge and understanding of both time periods.

Relevant points may include:

- Watchmen were used in both periods to prevent crime.
- The local community was responsible for arrests in both time periods. To do this they employed parish constables in the medieval period and town constables in the early modern period.
- From the later medieval period, Justices of the Peace (JPs) heard cases of minor local crimes. They were generally local lords. This continued in early modern England.
- The hue and cry was used in both periods because there was no national police force.

Hint

Look at this sample answer to Question 3. Refer back to the notes above, then look to see how some of the points are used here.

Q3: sample answer

One way in which the role of local communities in law enforcement was similar was that the hue and cry was still essential for catching criminals. In medieval England, people had to come out and join the chase of a criminal if the hue and cry was raised, or they would face a fine. Similarly, in the early modern period, there was still no police force. Even though there were town constables who had the power to arrest criminals, there weren't enough of them to effectively catch criminals. Consequently, the community was still expected to support them by joining in the hue and cry.

Similarity identified at start and linked to topic.

Examples are relevant, specific and accurate.

Language shows comparison made.

Key terms show strong understanding of topic.

Similarity explained wi
examples from each p

A very strong answer because...

This answer clearly identifies a similarity between the two time periods that is linked to the question topic. T student then gives specific and accurate examples from each period, focusing on how they were similar. The supporting information is balanced and relevant, and the answer is kept concise.

Explain why there were changes in the role of the Church in crime and punishment in the period c1000–c1700.

(12 marks)

You may use the following in your answer:

- Church courts
- heresy

You **must** also use information of your own.

Hint

Read the notes below, then look at the sample answer that follows.

Writing a good answer

Good answers will:

- give an analytical explanation which is tightly focused on the question throughout
- keep their explanation clear and well-organised throughout
- include information that is accurate, relevant and closely linked to the question
- show a wide range of knowledge and understanding of the topic.

Relevant points may include:

- The Church was responsible for trials for the crime of heresy. With the change of religion in England under the Tudors, punishing this crime became more important.
- Trial by ordeal was common until it was ended in 1215, which reduced the direct involvement of priests in deciding guilt or innocence in trials.
- Benefit of clergy was weakened in the 1500s and from 1576 Church courts did not try criminal cases, which meant that the Church courts became less important.
- Sanctuary in the medieval period could protect a criminal from trial, but became less important and was eventually abolished by 1623.
- Royal power increased following the English Reformation which meant that the monarch, as head of the Church, had more authority than Church leaders.

Q4: sample answer

Hint

Look at this sample answer to Question 4. Refer back to the notes above, then look to see how some of the points are used here.

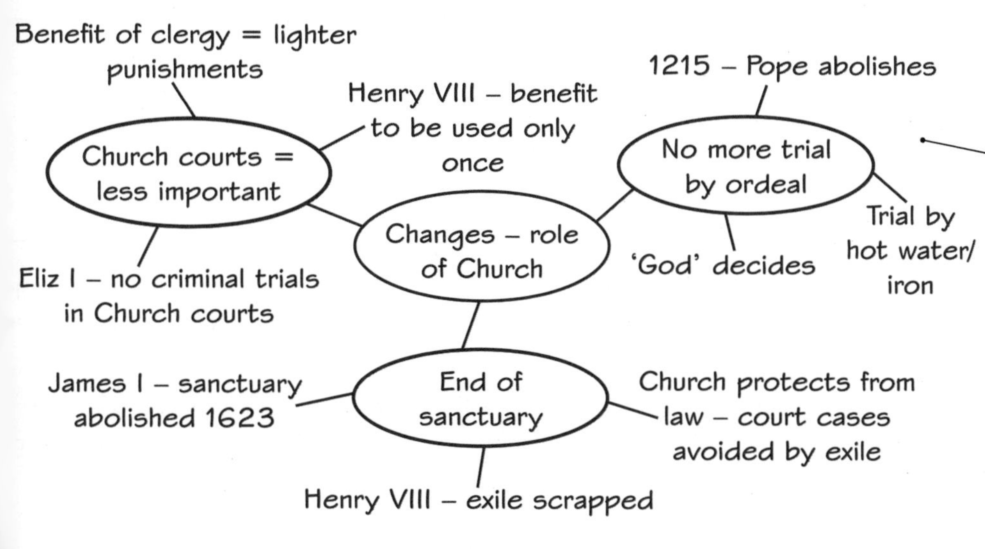

Quick plan helps to make answer clear and focused.

PEEL (Point – Evidence – Explain – Link) used to give clear structure in every paragraph.

Clear focus on time period given in question.

Relevant and accurate information used as evidence to support point.

Each reason clearly signposted, making whole answer well-organised.

Use of key term shows strong knowledge of topic.

Shows accurate and relevant knowledge and understanding of the topic.

Language used shows writing is analytical – shows answer is explaining why.

Answer tightly focused on question throughout.

One reason that the role of the Church in crime and punishment changed in the period c1000–c1700 was that Church courts became less important. In medieval England, anyone could claim benefit of clergy by reciting the 'neck verse'. This meant they could be tried at a Church court, where punishments were usually lighter, rather than a secular court. However, Henry VIII changed the law so a person could only use benefit of clergy once. Then, in 1576, Elizabeth I removed criminal trials from Church courts completely. Consequently, even though punishments for those claiming benefit of clergy were still decided by a Church court by 1600 the Church could no longer try people for crimes. Therefore, by 1700 the Church had a much smaller role in crime and punishment.

A second reason that the role of the Church changed was because of trial by ordeal. In Norman England, the Church had a lot of influence over crime and punishment because it managed trials by ordeal. When someone's guilt or innocence had not been decided by a secular court, the Church used various trials, such as trial by hot water or by hot iron, so that 'God' would decide. Trial by ordeal was abolished by the Pope in 1215. As a result, the Church no longer decided people's guilt or innocence in this way. This meant that the Church became far less involved in criminal trials, which changed the role of the Church in crime and punishment.

Three reasons given overall – including this one from own knowledge.

A third reason that the role of the Church changed was that sanctuary ended. In the medieval period, a person accused of a crime could flee to a church where they were protected from the law. This made the Church influential as the use of sanctuary could delay court cases or even avoid them completely if a criminal agreed to leave the country. Henry VIII removed the option for people to choose exile abroad as a way of avoiding court. As a result, sanctuary was weakened and James I ended it completely in 1623. Consequently, the Church had less influence over trials and its role in crime and punishment became less important.

Key term shows detailed knowledge of the topic.

Specific detail shows wide range of topic knowledge.

Explains why the reason caused the consequence in the question.

Links back to the question.

A very strong ·swer because...

·is answer is clear and well-organised. It gives three different, clear reasons, including two from the student's ·wn knowledge. For each point, the student provides relevant and accurate supporting evidence, then explains ·ow this led to changes in the role of the Church. Analytical language such as 'As a result...', 'This meant ·at' and 'Consequently...' shows the student is linking each reason back to the question. The answer is well ·ructured, with clear PEEL paragraphs, which keeps the answer tightly focused on the question and makes it ·asy to follow.

Hint

Read the notes below, then look at the sample answer on page 72.

Hint

Remember – in the exam you only need to answer **either** Question 5 **or** Question 6.

Answer EITHER Question 5 OR Question 6.
Spelling, punctuation, grammar and use of specialist terminology will be assessed in this question.

5 'The move towards prevention was the most important change to law enforcement in the years c1700–present.'

How far do you agree? Explain your answer.

(16 marks plus 4 marks for SPaG a use of specialist terminolo

You may use the following in your answer:

- Bow Street Runners
- Neighbourhood Watch

You **must** also use information of your own.

Writing a good answer

Good answers will:

- give an analytical explanation which is tightly focused on the issue in the question throughout
- keep their explanation clear and well-organised throughout
- include information that is accurate, relevant and closely linked to the question
- show a wide range of knowledge and understanding of the topic
- reach an overall judgement which is fully justified
- use correct spelling, punctuation and grammar and specialist terms.

Relevant points that support the statement may include:

- Prevention has been an important change throughout the period, including the patrols by the Bow Street Runners in the 1700s and by beat constables in London in the 1800s.
- Neighbourhood Watch organisations developed from 1982 have helped to prevent crimes in communities.
- PCSOs build community relationships and make the police more visible, which helps to prevent crime.
- Anti-crime poster campaigns and programmes like Prevent are specifically designed to reduce crime and a helping to challenge extremism and radicalisation.

Relevant points that counter the statement may include:

- Until the mid-1700s, there was no police force and the law was enforced by local militia and watchmen, but in 1749 Henry Fielding set up the Bow Street Runners, which was an important first effort to introduce a professional police force.
- Robert Peel built on this idea with the creation of the Metropolitan Police in 1829, which led to a new type law enforcement – a centralised police force.
- The 1856 Police Act meant that by the mid-1800s every town and country had to have a professional poli force and this was controlled by the government, fundamentally changing how policing was organised.
- In the earlier part of the period, the focus was more about stopping crime rather than solving it. After the creation of the CID in 1878, the role of the detective was developed, helped in the twentieth century by technology and specialised units.

Q5: sample answer

Plan:

Support	Challenge
1. Prevention methods • Neighbourhood Watch • PCSOs • Building community relationships	2. Dev. of local police forces • Met. Police 1829 • Police Act 1856 • Gov. in charge 3. Dev. of detective role • CID created 1878 • New technology e.g. DNA • Not just stopping – solving
Judgement: Partially agree – prevention important but local forces changed whole system	

The move towards prevention has been an important change in law enforcement in the years c1700–present. For example, programmes like Neighbourhood Watch were created to prevent crime. However, I only partially agree with the statement as there were other important changes in this period. Overall, I think the most important change was the development of local police forces.

There are examples of prevention in the 1700s, with the Bow Street Runners who patrolled major roads to discourage highwaymen, and beat constables in the 1800s in London, who patrolled high crime areas like Whitechapel, but the move towards prevention has been especially important in the last 40 years. An example of this is the development of Neighbourhood Watch groups from 1982 which, since 2002, have been supported by the recruitment of PCSOs. The aim of Neighbourhood Watch is to help the police by preventing crimes in local communities. Instead of arresting criminals, like regular police officers, PCSOs aim to build relationships within the community, and also make the police more visible in high crime areas, so that people are less likely to commit crimes. For example, PCSOs often ride on public transport, which is a common scene of antisocial crime. These methods of prevention have been quite successful so are an important change to law enforcement since 1700.

Hint

Look at this sample answer to Question 5. Refer back to the notes on page 71, then look to see how some of the points are used here.

Effective plan helps to keep answer clear, well-structured and focused.

Including a judgement in plan helps keep the whole answer focused.

Short introduction says what answer will discuss and gives clear judgement on the opinion in the statement.

Sticks to date range given in question.

Language used shows writing is analytical and giving a judgement.

Paragraph starts with a point focused on the question.

Shows detailed knowledge and understanding of a factor given in question.

Includes specific examples of accurate evidence.

Explains how the factor caused the change – the move to prevention – in the question, and links back to question.

Beginning of counter-argument clearly signposted.

Language shows analysis and gives a judgement about the statement in the question.

Uses own knowledge to discuss a factor not included in the question.

Accurate spelling, punctuation and grammar throughout.

Detailed own knowledge used to explain point being discussed – development of local police forces.

Judgement made clear throughout answer.

Gives a reason for judgement.

Language clearly signposts a new example will be discussed.

Makes links between factors.

Use of key terms throughout shows strong understanding of topic.

Accurate use of subject terminology.

Language used shows writing is analytical – it is explaining why.

However, although I agree that the move to prevention has been important, the development of local police forces has been a more significant change. In the 1700s, there was no police force, and instead local militia were used to put down riots, while local watchmen dealt with petty criminals. In 1749, the first effort to introduce a professional police force was made, when Henry Fielding set up the Bow Street Runners. Robert Peel then improved on this idea when he created the Metropolitan Police force in 1829. By 1856, the Police Act meant that every town and county had to set up a local police force. This meant that by the mid-nineteenth century there were professional organisations which answered to the government, via the Home Secretary, rather than local magistrates being responsible for keeping law and order. In my view, this was therefore a fundamental change to law enforcement because it affected the whole way policing was organised.

Another important change was the development of the role of the detective. In 1878, the CID was set up in the Met Police to solve crimes. The Bow Street Runners had attempted to develop the detective role in the 1700s but without much success and, initially, the CID was not very successful either, as they had limited technology. However, in the twentieth century detectives became a more effective part of law enforcement, which was partly due to new technology, like DNA testing and CCTV. Consequently, these developments have allowed detectives to be more effective in solving crimes as well as just stopping them. Therefore, the work of detectives has been an important change to law enforcement.

Regularly links back to question.

Conclusion is clearly signposted.

Overall, I partially agree with the statement, because it is true that the move to prevention has been important, with the Bow Street Runners and beat constables but especially in the last 40 years. A major role of law enforcement through the whole period has been preventing crime. However, the most fundamental change has been the setting up of local police forces. This entirely changed the basis of policing from local communities to the government overseeing law enforcement through professional organisations. Also, the other changes, like prevention and detective work, have been carried out through these local police forces. Consequently, I think the most important change to law enforcement has been the creation of local police forces between 1829 and 1856.

Conclusion gives clear, overall judgement.

Conclusion briefly compares factors discussed in answer.

Judgement is fully justified with reasons.

A very strong ɩswer because...

ɩis answer is well organised, taking each change in turn, and remaining analytical and focused on the question. ɩe student considers the argument in the statement before looking at the arguments against it. Each point is ɩpported with good topic knowledge and a clear understanding of the key changes in law enforcement. The ɩudent uses accurate spelling, punctuation and grammar and specialist terms throughout. The student comes ɩ a judgement on which of the changes is most important, following this line of argument throughout the ɩswer, and gives reasons for their decision in the conclusion.

Hint

Read the notes below, then look at the sample answer on page 76.

Hint

Remember – in the exam you only need to answer **either** Question 5 **or** Question 6.

Answer EITHER Question 5 OR Question 6.
Spelling, punctuation, grammar and use of specialist terminology will be assessed in this question.

6 'Crimes against property were the greatest challenge to the government in the period c1000–c1700.'

How far do you agree? Explain your answer.

(16 marks plus 4 marks for SPaG and use of specialist terminology)

You may use the following in your answer:

- poaching
- the Gunpowder Plot (1605)

You **must** also use information of your own.

Writing a good answer

Good answers will:

- give an analytical explanation which is tightly focused on the issue in the question throughout
- keep their explanation clear and well-organised throughout
- include information that is accurate, relevant and closely linked to the question
- show a wide range of knowledge and understanding of the topic
- reach an overall judgement which is fully justified
- use correct spelling, punctuation and grammar and specialist terms.

Relevant points that support the statement may include:

- Poaching was a common crime against property – specifically against landowners – which presented a challe throughout the period, at a time when there was no professional police force.
- Poaching was particularly an issue with the introduction of the Forest Laws, as hunting in Royal Forests beca a crime against royal property.
- Smuggling became a problem later in the period, particularly the 1600s. As smuggling involved people avoic import taxes, it meant the government lost income.
- Both poaching and smuggling were social crimes, accepted by the majority of people. They were common a hard to prevent.

Relevant points that counter the statement may include:

- Crimes against authority, such as treason and rebellion, were often a dangerous challenge in this period, ev though they weren't as common as crimes against property.
- The Gunpowder Plot of 1605 is an example of treason, which challenged the government by threatening the of the king.
- Rebellions also presented a challenge to government authority in this period, for example the rebellions of Anglo-Saxon earls against William I.
- In the 1500s, vagabondage was a crime that the government struggled to deal with. Although the Vagranc Act was introduced in 1547, it was later repealed because it was impossible to enforce.

Q6: sample answer

Plan:

Support	Challenge
1. Poaching • Forest Laws – hunting = crime • Enclosure = more poaching • Social crime – 'acceptable' 2. Smuggling • More common in 1600s • Supported by many	3. Treason • Threat to government • Gunpowder Plot 1605 • Danger to monarchy 4. Rebellion • Anglo-Saxons vs. William I • Revolts against Tudor religious changes • Against authority
Judgement: Mainly agree – property crimes more common even though crimes against authority more dangerous	

Crimes against property were a constant challenge to the government in the years c1000–c1700. For example, poaching was a very common crime, and the government and landowners struggled to prevent it. There were also other challenges for the government, like treason and rebellion. However, although these were more dangerous to the government, they were also rare, so overall I agree that crimes against property were the greatest challenge in this period.

One example of a crime against property throughout this period was poaching. This involved people hunting on land without permission. It became a crime in Norman England, when William I created the Royal Forests. Since the Anglo-Saxons depended on hunting for food, they were forced to poach to provide for their families, but this was now a crime against royal property. This crime continued throughout the medieval period and became more common in the years c1500–c1700, when landlords began to enclose common land, which meant there was even less land for people to hunt on legally. As a result, poaching was a challenge to the government as it was such a common crime, and it affected the property of members of the government, who were landlords. However, it was also a social crime, which meant that most people thought it was acceptable. Without professional police forces it was hard for local magistrates to prevent it, even if they caught some poachers. This made it a real challenge for the government because they had no effective way of stopping it from happening.

Hint

Look at this sample answer to Question 6. Refer back to the notes on page 75, then look to see how some of the points are used here.

Effective plan helps to keep answer clear, well-structured and focused.

Introduces the other factors that will be discussed.

Introduction gives a clear judgement on the opinion in the statement.

Begins with an example of the main factor in the statement.

Shows detailed knowledge and understanding of topic.

Includes specific and accurate evidence.

Language used shows writing is analytical – it is explaining why.

Explains why the factor was a challenge.

Links back to the question.

Language clearly signposts second example will be discussed.

Sticks to date range given in question.

Makes links between factors.

Language used shows writing is analytical and giving a judgement.

Regularly links back to question.

Another example of a crime against property that challenged the government was smuggling. This became common in the seventeenth century, when the government increased taxes on imported goods such as brandy and tea. Like poaching, most people considered smuggling an acceptable social crime, and many even thought it was heroic, as the smugglers provided people with cheap goods that allowed them to avoid paying high import taxes. As a result, many people benefitted from this crime and so were often willing to help the smugglers to hide. Therefore, smuggling is another example that shows that crimes against property were a major challenge for the government, who were losing income because of it.

Beginning of counter-argument clearly signposted.

Accurate spelling, punctuation and grammar throughout.

Uses the second bullet point given in the question to add to counter-argument.

Uses accurate subject knowledge as evidence.

However, although it is true that crimes against property were the most common challenge to the government, they were not the only challenging crimes, and some were more dangerous. An example of a more dangerous challenge is the crime of treason, which is where individuals make plots against the government or monarch. An example of this is the Gunpowder Plot of 1605, when a group of Catholics planned to blow up Parliament and James I. This was therefore a crime against authority, and it could have killed the King of England. Consequently, although not as common as crimes against property, treason was a significant challenge to the government.

Uses own knowledge to discuss a factor not included in the question.

Detailed own knowledge used to explain impact of factor being discussed – rebellion.

Accurate use of subject terminology and spelled correctly.

Explains why this factor was important.

Like treason, another example of a crime against authority in this period was rebellion. For example, in Norman England, Anglo-Saxon earls led rebellions against William I which forced him to use his army to defend his control of England. Similarly, when the Tudor monarchs changed between Catholicism and Protestantism in the 1500s, there were several violent rebellions against the government. If these rebellions had succeeded, they could have potentially overthrown the government. As a result, they were a more dangerous challenge to the government than crimes against property.

Language shows analysis and gives a judgement about this factor.

Language clearly signposts start of conclusion.

In conclusion, I mainly agree with the statement. It is true that there were more dangerous crimes which challenged the government, like rebellion and treason, but in the 700 years of this period, they did not happen often and the government was always able to stop them. In contrast, poaching was a constant crime against landowners which the government was unable to prevent, and smuggling in the later years was also a common crime which was essentially unpreventable. Consequently, crimes against property were the greatest challenge to the government in the years c1000–c1700.

Conclusion summarises argument and comes to an overall judgement.

Compares factors and gives a clear reason for judgement.

A very strong answer because...

A clear judgement is given in the introduction, which is then followed throughout the answer. The analysis covers arguments for and against the statement in the question, and the counter-argument is clearly signposted. The student uses their own knowledge to support their argument, and points are backed up with relevant and accurate evidence. Examples from across the full date range are given. The conclusion offers an overall judgement that is fully justified with reasons. The plan the student made helped them to produce an answer that is well-organised throughout. There is a good quality of spelling, punctuation and grammar, with lots of examples of specialist terminology.

Answers

Where an exemplar answer is given, this is not necessarily the only correct response. In most cases there is a range of responses that can gain full marks.

KNOWLEDGE BOOSTER

1. Medieval England

1 Any one from:
- Murder
- Assault
- Public disorder
- Rape

2 Any two from:
- Arson
- Theft (like poaching or stealing)
- Counterfeiting

3 Any one from:
- Treason
- Rebellion
- Heresy

4 B

5 Any two from:
- Village communities were evicted.
- Only those who paid for hunting rights could hunt – poorer people could not afford this and some went hungry or had to break the law.
- Hunting without a license became illegal so many Saxons were punished.
- Grazing animals without a license became illegal so those who could not afford a license could not afford to keep animals.
- Collecting wood without a license became illegal meaning poorer people struggled to keep warm and cook food.

6 If an Anglo-Saxon murdered a Norman and was not caught, a fine was paid by the Anglo-Saxons in the hundred where the murder occurred.

7 Aiii; Bii; Ci; Dv; Eiv

2. Medieval England

8

	Norman England	Later medieval England
Continuity	At least one from: • Hue and cry • Tithings • Court system • Trial by ordeal	At least one from: • Hue and cry • Tithings • Trial by combat
Change	At least one from: • Trial by combat • Foresters • Castles	At least one from: • Role of parish constable • Role of night watch • End of trial by ordeal or combat • Role of Justice of the Peace, knights and sheriffs

9 Punishment by execution

10 Punishment by physical pain

11 Any one from:
- Anglo-Saxon Wergild fines cost more if the victim was wealthier.
- Medieval execution methods were different for rich and poor.
- Priests were tried in Church courts and punished less harshly.

12 Ai; Biii; Cii

3. Early modern England

1 B

2 Having religious beliefs different to the official beliefs of the religion.

3 A. True; B. False – people feared and disliked vagabonds; C. True; D. False – people feared witches and witchcraft; E. True

4 Any two from:
- Benefit of clergy could be used only once.
- Serious crimes were no longer tried by Church courts.
- From 1576 only moral crimes could be tried by Church courts.
- By 1623 sanctuary had been abolished.

5 A

4. Early modern England

6 Any two from:
- Pillory/stocks
- Flogging
- Maiming
- Hanging
- Fines

7 Any one from:
- It was meant to act as a deterrent.
- The public wanted serious punishments that still allowed rehabilitation rather than execution.
- Many people thought execution was too harsh for petty criminals.
- It provided workers for the American colonies.

8 A4; B1; C3; D7; E6; F2; G5; H8

9
- It caused bad harvests – people wanted scapegoats.
- It weakened the control of local authorities.
- It increased religious differences – Puritans believed Catholics practised witchcraft.

Plus any two from:
- Many women were alone as husbands had left to fight.
- More strangers appeared as they moved around due to the war.
- Individuals like Matthew Hopkins instigated witch-hunts.

10 Any two from:
- He hunted witches.
- His work led to about 300 investigations and 112 hangings.
- He caused panic through trials and pamphlets.

5. 18th- and 19th-century Britain

1 Any one from:
- Street theft and burglary increased.
- Poaching increased as large-scale poaching gangs formed.
- Highway robbery increased.
- Smuggling increased and large smuggling gangs moved huge quantities of goods.

2 Any one from:
- More people were travelling, which increased opportunities for highway robbery.
- Increased trade meant more goods and money were on the roads, which increased the temptation to rob people on the road.
- Many roads were isolated so it was fairly easy to get away with highway robbery.
- There was more poverty so more people were driven to crime.
- Highway robbery was a social crime and seen as acceptable by many, so people were more willing to take the risk.

3 A. True; B. False – they were protesting low wages; C. False – they were sentenced to transportation; D. True; E. True.

4
- Before 1700, there was no police force. Towns appointed watchmen.
- In the early 1700s, there was continuity in who dealt with crime. <u>Watchmen and parish constables dealt with local crime. Soldiers dealt with riots.</u>
- In 1749, Henry Fielding <u>created the Bow Street Runners, a London-based force which patrolled major roads and investigated crimes.</u>
- In 1829 <u>the Metropolitan Police were formed in London, the first professional force.</u>
- In 1856 <u>the Police Act forced all towns and counties to have professional police forces.</u>

6. 18th- and 19th-century Britain

5 During the 1800s, more people began to feel that punishments should <u>equal</u> the crime. The use of the death penalty <u>decreased</u> as more people believed <u>capital</u> punishment was inhumane except for very serious crimes. The use of transportation and imprisonment therefore <u>increased</u>.

6 John Howard, Elizabeth Fry

7 The idea of keeping prisoners separate inside prison so that they did not communicate or mix.

8 Any two from:
- It was thought to allow prisoners time to reflect on their crimes and reform.
- Prisoners would not be influenced by other criminals.
- The isolation was seen as an appropriate punishment.
- It was believed to be a deterrent.

9 Reforming the penal code – at least one from:
- Reduced number of capital crimes by over 100
- Less harsh punishments for petty crimes
- Focus on reform, not just punishment

Prison reform – at least one from:
- 1823 Gaols Act passed
- Chaplains regularly visited prisoners
- Gaolers paid
- No chains in prison

Metropolitan Police Act, 1829 – at least one from:
- Centralised police force created
- Uniforms identified professional law enforcement officers
- Reduced street crime and disorder
- Officers trained to avoid use of force

7. Modern Britain

1 B

2 Any one from:
- Violent crimes use new weapons.
- Modern vehicles are now used instead of horses (for example, driving a car while drunk is now illegal as was driving a horse-drawn coach while drunk).
- Fraud and theft can be internet-based.
- Terrorism uses modern vehicles and weapons and is more of a risk to ordinary people.
- Smuggling includes people-trafficking.

3

New crimes	Details
Race crime	• New race crimes were defined by the 1968 Race Relations Act and 2006 Racial and Religious Hatred Act. At least one from: • Crimes classed as 'hate' crimes can be given more severe sentences.
Drug crime	At least one from: • The 1971 Misuse of Drugs Act made taking or supplying some substances illegal. • The criminalisation of drugs is controversial.
Driving offences	At least one from: • It is illegal to drive while under the influence of drugs. • It is illegal to drive without insurance, an MOT certificate or a valid driving licence. • It is illegal to drive while using a mobile phone. • It is illegal to break the speed limit. • It is illegal to ignore traffic lights and road signs.

4 A. True; B. True; C. False – some police units are now armed; D. False – Neighbourhood Watches are made up of local volunteers.

5 Any two from:
- Radios
- CCTV
- Computers
- Vehicles
- Finger printing
- DNA evidence

8. Modern Britain

6 Any two from:
- Different types of prisons for different types of criminals, for example open prisons, high-security prisons.
- Hard labour and corporal punishment have been abolished in prisons.
- Prisons for young offenders have been set up.
- There is more education and training in prisons.
- Women's prisons are different to men's prisons.

7 Any two from:
- Community sentences
- ASBOs
- Electronic tagging

8 Someone who has religious, moral or political objections to war.

9 Aiii; Bi; Cii

10 Any one from:
- Craig, not Bentley, fired the gun.
- Bentley did not hold the gun.
- Bentley was detained by the wounded police officer at the time that Craig killed the second police officer.
- Bentley had a learning disability and a mental age of 10.

11 Any two from:
- It showed the big differences in sentences given for murder, as Bentley was hanged but Craig was sentenced to prison.
- It showed that the Home Secretary's authority to reprieve murderers was not used consistently.
- The case received a lot of sympathetic media coverage and triggered a huge public outcry about the sentence.
- It increased the number of people who were opposed to capital punishment.
- It helped lead to changes in the law regarding sentences for murder.

9. Whitechapel, c1870–c1900

1 A. True; B. False – beat constables patrolled a set route of streets to prevent crime; C. True; D. False – they answered to the Home Secretary E. False – many working-class people feared and disliked the police.

2 • Overcrowding

Plus at least five from:
- Extreme poverty
- High unemployment
- People would do anything to avoid the workhouse (which was seen as a last resort due to the conditions there)
- Tensions between ethnic groups
- High levels of prostitution
- High rates of alcoholism

3 In Whitechapel, a large part of the population lived in temporary accommodation. A common place to stay was in lodging houses. Because people moved a lot, there was no sense of community.

4 Any two from:
- Immigrants were forced to accept low paid work in sweatshops which annoyed other workers.
- Many immigrants were Jewish and anti-Semitism was common.
- People often associated immigrants with dangerous, revolutionary ideas.
- People tended to associate all Irish immigrants with the Fenians, a movement that used violence.
- 'Foreigners' were blamed for the Ripper murders.
- People blamed immigrants for overcrowding in Whitechapel.

10. Whitechapel, c1870–1900

5 Answers will depend on your own judgement. The key thing is to have clear reasons for the choices you make.

6 • Searching houses, pubs and opium dens

Plus any three from:
- Distributing leaflets
- Advertising in newspapers
- Following up clues/evidence
- Following up post-mortems and coroners' reports
- Producing annotated sketches of crime scenes
- Taking photographs
- Setting up soup kitchens to encourage the poor to help the police
- Interviewing suspects

7 Any two from:
- The Bertillon system of measuring and photographing suspects improved record-keeping.
- Central records for the Met Police meant information could be shared more easily.
- Telephones made communication faster.

8 Any three from:
- Media coverage attracted hoax letters.
- Coverage led to thousands of wild theories.
- Coverage stirred up racial tensions and increased violent crimes.
- The media criticised the police.

9 Any one from:
- The Whitechapel Vigilance Committee disrupted the police investigation by organising its own patrols and rewards.
- The rivalry between the Met and the City of London police forces meant that they competed with each other, rather than cooperating to solve the case.

Notes

Notes

Notes

Notes